OneNote® 2013

FOR DUMMIES®

A Wiley Brand

OneNote® 2013

FOR DUMMIES®

A Wiley Brand

by James H. Russell

FOR DUMMIES®

A Wiley Brand

About the Author

James Russell has built and repaired PCs and installed, configured, and debugged most versions of Windows from Windows 3.1.1 for Workgroups to Windows 8. He began using OneNote in its initial release more than a decade ago and has loved the app ever since. He is a longtime editor and writer of technical books for John Wiley & Sons and other publishers. His latest book prior to *OneNote 2013 For Dummies* is *Windows 8 Kickstart* for McGraw-Hill. He is currently integrating social media strategy as a career focus and was recently named by Mashable.com as one of 101 social media experts to follow on Google+. James has had significant experience with the Mozilla open-source project since Mozilla's M4 milestone in 1999, having been responsible for Netscape 6's View Theme menu. He also rewrote the Linux and Windows release notes and README files for Mozilla's .6 and 1.0 releases. You can find and follow James at @Kovu_ on Twitter or by looking him up by name on Facebook and Google+.

Dedication

To my sister Julie Mae Donovan: *Always my touchtone, Emma.*

Author's Acknowledgments

First and foremost, I thank my amazing agent Carole Jelen, who pushed for me to have the chance to write a proposal for this book; and Steve Hayes, senior acquisitions editor at Wiley, for giving me extra time to prepare a proposal and for accepting said proposal. Thank you two for believing in me and giving me the opportunity to write a *For Dummies* book on a product I adore. Thanks are also due to Kara Berman and Melissa Dingle Hood at Waggener Edstrom Worldwide for helping me with general questions and for getting me Windows Phone screenshots. A special shout out also to Samantha Kristine for providing me with the screen shot of the Nexus 7 version of OneNote with absolutely *zero* notice.

Secondly, I've been an editor and sometime writer for John Wiley & Sons since March 1999 (then IDG Books Worldwide), and I wouldn't be writing this book if it weren't for a lot of IDGB/Wiley folks who've believed in me and helped me grow as an editor and as a writer over the last 14 years. Specifically, thanks are due to Leah Michael, Kyle Looper, Jodi Jensen, Kathryn Bourgoine, Jade Leah Williams, Andy Cummings, the "two Marys" Mary Bednarek and Mary C. Corder, Mark Enochs, Nicole Haims, Katie Feltman, Cherie Case, Melba Hopper, Sharon Mealka, and Megan Saur.

As is usually the case with writers, many people who didn't help me write the book per se still helped me survive, stay centered, and were patient with me while I wrote and midwifed the book, and those people are due nods, as well. Specifically, thanks of course to my mother, Jacquelyn Arlene Cordoza, and my late father, John Howard Russell — I wouldn't be me or here to write this book without you. Thanks also to my good friends Nancy Ciarrocchi and David Youhanna for all you've both done for me.

Publisher's Acknowledgments

We're proud of this book; please send us your comments at `http://dummies.custhelp.com`. For other comments, please contact our Customer Care Department within the U.S. at 877-762-2974, outside the U.S. at 317-572-3993, or fax 317-572-4002.

Some of the people who helped bring this book to market include the following:

Acquisitions, Editorial, and Vertical Websites

Sr. Project Editor: Mark Enochs

Executive Editor: Steve Hayes

Copy Editor: Melba Hopper

Technical Editor: Sharon Mealka

Editorial Manager: Leah Michael

Vertical Websites Project Manager: Laura Moss-Hollister

Supervising Producer: Rich Graves

Vertical Websites Associate Producers: Josh Frank, Marilyn Hummel, Douglas Kuhn, Shawn Patrick

Editorial Assistant: Annie Sullivan

Sr. Editorial Assistant: Cherie Case

Cover Photos: © ПетрСтепанов/ iStockphoto for icon; Circle © John Takai / iStockphoto

Composition Services

Project Coordinator: Katie Crocker

Layout and Graphics: Carrie A. Cesavice, Jennifer Creasey, Joyce Haughey

Proofreader: Toni Settle

Indexer: BIM Indexing & Proofreading Services

Publishing and Editorial for Technology Dummies

  Richard Swadley, Vice President and Executive Group Publisher

  Andy Cummings, Vice President and Publisher

  Mary Bednarek, Executive Acquisitions Director

  Mary C. Corder, Editorial Director

Publishing for Consumer Dummies

  Kathy Nebenhaus, Vice President and Executive Publisher

Composition Services

  Debbie Stailey, Director of Composition Services

Contents at a Glance

Table of Contents

Introduction

*O*neNote celebrates its tenth birthday with Office 2013, and finally I get to offer you an accompanying *For Dummies* book! OneNote has come a long way from its beginnings in Windows XP Tablet PC Edition. It's become a powerful super-app that allows you not only to take notes but also to consolidate other Office content, and now you can even access your notes on all major smartphones and tablets whether or not they run a version of Windows. With OneNote Mobile for Android and iOS, the OneNote Web App, click-to-run versions for Office 365, and the Windows 8 version of OneNote, suddenly OneNote is everywhere.

All told, Microsoft's pet Office app of yore that so many loved but few publishers thought was worthy of a book has really grown up and achieved critical mass with the 2013 release. So welcome, friend, to the-long-lost-but-now-a-reality *OneNote 2013 For Dummies!*

Foolish Assumptions

Foolish as I am, I make assumptions. I kind of have to, actually; if not, I'd have to write a tome describing the fundamentals on how to use a computer, a smartphone, a tablet, and basic applications for all these devices — and you wouldn't buy the book because it would be so expensive and off-topic. So I assume.

Following is specifically what I assume about you, gentle reader, as I write this book:

- ✔ You have used a PC of some kind in the past, preferably running Windows 7 or Windows 8, as well as Windows apps.

- ✔ You have used the Internet at some point in your jolly existence on this mud ball we call Earth.

- ✔ You know what touchscreens, smartphones, and tablets are and how they work in general.

- ✔ You know that Android is an operating system from Google that runs on smartphones and tablets.

- ✔ You know that iOS is an operating system from Apple that runs on iPhones, iPads, and iPod touches.

Foolish assumptions done with. Groovy. Moving on . . .

Conventions Used in This Book

This book uses two major text effects, one for typing items on your keyboard and one for computer output or hyperlinks within text. When I want you to type something, I use bold, as in, "In the Blah field, type **your monkey was a wookiee**." URLs and computer output appear like this, respectively: www.microsoft.com and www.facebook.com/onenotefordummies.

Also, because OneNote is on many platforms and now, with Windows 8, Windows is on touchscreens, the term "click" is no longer appropriate. Instead, you'll see that I write "click or tap" and "right-click or press and hold on" to include instructions for both keyboard/mouse and touch interfaces.

A happy tale of your author and OneNote

In early 2002 while an in-house development editor at Wiley in Indianapolis, I gave a presentation to Wiley editors and brass on what I considered the future: How I was editing via pen marking up PDF chapters using a Wacom Intuos 2 tablet and Adobe Acrobat 5. Later that year, I bought a slightly used Acer tablet PC running Windows XP Tablet PC Edition — including the first version of OneNote. I fell in love with both the concept of the tablet and the OneNote app. Unfortunately, tablet PCs didn't have touchscreen capabilities and were just not "there" as tablet devices.

In late 2012, my agent pings me via e-mail that Wiley is interested in seeing a proposal from me on *OneNote 2013 For Dummies* — I'd often wondered whether that book would ever be written. My proposal was accepted (yay!), and I started writing the book.

Fast forward a little further to mid-February 2013 at which time I have three chapters of *OneNote 2013 For Dummies* left to write — including the stuff on ink. Amazingly, I score a Surface Pro (a device I've coveted for years) in the first available batch from Microsoft just in time to write the ink-related content for the book — which can't be properly written on anything other than a Surface Pro or a similar device.

So now I'm finishing up writing a book I've wanted to see for a decade using a machine I've wanted for as long. Can you say geek fate? I can.

Icons Used in This Book

I use a few standard icons in the book to visually call out information that's especially useful or noteworthy. Specifically, *OneNote 2013 For Dummies* uses the following icons.

Tips call out information that can save you time, is especially cool, or both. Read these to get the most out of the various versions of OneNote.

I use this icon when referring to something I want you to keep in mind or to remind you of something mentioned in earlier chapters.

This icon points out techie stuff that you may not want to bother reading but may find interesting if you do.

These icons aren't to be ignored; if you see one, read it because it can save you some kind of trauma in regard to your notes — such as losing them or the content within them.

How This Book Is Organized

This book is divided into logical parts and chapters to help you know where to look for the information you need. The following sections describe the book's four parts.

Part I: Getting Started with OneNote 2013

In this part, I get you up to speed with OneNote 2013, which is the most feature-rich version of OneNote. Early chapters orient you to the software, while later chapters describe more intermediate topics.

Part II: Taking Notes via Other OneNote Versions

With OneNote 2013, the software is now complemented by several mobile versions of OneNote plus a Windows 8 version that overhauls the way you use OneNote — or any Windows app, for that matter — as well as versions for Android and iOS devices and OneNote Web

App, which runs on any device that can access real (not mobile) web pages. This part gives you the skinny on all these versions.

Although Windows Phone isn't covered much in this book, the functionality of the Windows Phone version of OneNote is most similar to the Android version of OneNote. Although all the instructions in Chapter 7 may not be accurate for OneNote on Windows Phone, the chapter will at least give you an idea about how to use OneNote on your Windows Phone.

Part III: Putting OneNote Through Its Paces

Sharing and collaborating are key features of OneNote, and the first chapter in this part shows you how to do so. The second chapter takes you through various fictional scenarios that show you how useful OneNote can be to helping you simplify your life whether you use the software at home, work, or school.

Part IV: The Part of Tens

Since the first *For Dummies* book *DOS For Dummies* by Dan Gookin, a staple of the series has been "The Part of Tens" chapters. In *OneNote 2013 For Dummies,* "The Part of Tens" chapters offer you ten cool resources and add-ins for OneNote as well as ten killer tips for using the software.

Where to Go from Here

For Dummies books include a Table of Contents at the beginning of the books and an Index at the back to help you easily look up topics you want to know about. From here, I suggest that you go to Chapter 1 if you've no idea how OneNote 2013 works. On the other hand, if you're using OneNote on a mobile device, see the chapter in Part II that covers your device.

This book is also more than just the pages between the covers. Because your author is a social media fiend, he's given the book a Twitter account (@OneNoteFD), a Facebook page, a Google+ page, and a Google+ community page — see Chapter 12 for more information and how to find these sites.

Occasionally there are updates for tech books, and if there are any for this book, you can find them at www.dummies.com/go/onenote2013fd.

Part I
Getting Started with OneNote 2013

In this part . . .

- ✔ Learn how to perform basic tasks in OneNote 2013.
- ✔ Find out how to manage and organize your notes and keep them secure.
- ✔ Read up on how to format your notes.
- ✔ Discover how to insert external data and take quick notes.
- ✔ Find out how you can sync with SkyDrive.

Chapter 1

OneNote Basics

In This Chapter

▶ Getting started with OneNote

▶ Making your first note

▶ Managing your notes

▶ Becoming familiar with the various OneNote interfaces

● ●

*M*any Microsoft Office suite applications have come and gone over the years, but none became one of the core Office apps alongside Word, Excel, and PowerPoint like OneNote has. Over the course of its decade in the Office suite, OneNote has become a killer application on many levels, and particularly OneNote 2013 with its SkyDrive cloud integration and instant sync. In addition, with versions on critical non-Microsoft platforms such as Apple's iOS and Google's Android, OneNote has been thrown into the spotlight.

In this chapter, I show you how to get up and running with OneNote, including how to sign in to the app with a Microsoft account, how to create new notes and manage them, and how to familiarize yourself with the app's interface.

Where OneNote came from

Microsoft originally created OneNote for the tablet PC, which ran Windows XP Tablet PC Edition, in Office 2003. The operating system was the first version of Windows to support the ability to write on a screen using a stylus using digital ink features, which is essentially a pen-like device without ink. OneNote was designed to take advantage of and show off these new stylus-based features. The initial targets for the new application were students taking notes in school, but as the years passed, OneNote became more feature-rich and diverse in terms of its utility, and with its ten-year anniversary release, OneNote has matured enough to appeal to far more people than just students.

Setting Up OneNote 2013

Office 2013, and thus OneNote, includes a new sign-in process that allows you to sync your Office settings across devices. Previous versions of OneNote and Office supported only the ability to include your name and initials in the applications' options so that you had a sort of "signature" for comments and tracked changes. By contrast, OneNote 2013, as well as other apps in the Office 2013 suite, includes a Windows-like sign-in interface with which you can sync settings across devices and even run OneNote on computers and devices that don't have the app installed.

If you use the same Microsoft account for Windows 8 and Office 2013, both Windows 8 and Office 2013 settings are synced via your SkyDrive across all Windows 8 or later devices that you log in to. Furthermore, you need to remember only one account name and password for both Windows and Office.

Getting a Microsoft account

With the release of Windows 8, Microsoft followed in the footsteps of its competitors Apple and Google and those companies' app stores by creating the Windows Store and tying it to a Microsoft account. A Microsoft e-mail account that functions as a single sign-on to all Microsoft services, including Windows 8, Office 2013, and Windows Store, with which all your downloaded apps will be associated so that you can access them on other Windows 8-compatible devices.

While not required, without a Microsoft account, you won't be able to use cool features like sync and SkyDrive across multiple devices — all of your apps and settings will be tied to a single computer.

Creating a brand-new Outlook.com account

At the same time that Office 2013 and Windows 8 were being finalized, Microsoft introduced a new e-mail service called Outlook. com. In similar fashion to Gmail, with an @outlook.com address you get 7G of free cloud storage via SkyDrive as well as integrated web app versions of Word, Excel, and PowerPoint. (OneNote has a web version tied to the app, not Outlook.com; I discuss the OneNote web app interface in Chapter 9.) In comparison to all other Microsoft e-mail accounts, which come with none of these features, Outlook.com clearly offers far more value.

Designed essentially as a competitor to Google Docs, Outlook.com web apps offer a more limited feature set than the full Office 2013 apps, but these features are nonetheless adequate for casual users.

You can set up an Outlook.com account at — surprise! — www.outlook.com. Here's how:

1. **Surf over to** www.outlook.com **with your web browser and click the Sign Up Now link.**

   A screen appears with empty text fields.

2. **Fill in your name, birth date, and gender under the Who Are You? heading.**

3. **Fill in a desired account name under the How Would You Like to Sign In? heading and then enter a password twice into the next two fields.**

4. **In the next section, enter at least two methods for Microsoft to identify you if you need to reset your password.**

   You can enter your phone number, add an alternate e-mail address, or click the Or Choose a Security Question link and choose a question and enter your answer.

5. **Choose your location and enter your ZIP code in the next section.**

6. **Enter the CAPTCHA code in the field, uncheck the check box below it if you don't want promotional e-mails, and click or tap the I Accept button.**

   A screen appears explaining a bit about your new account with a video you can watch if you choose to.

7. **Click or tap the Continue to Inbox button, and you're done.**

Upgrading an existing Microsoft account to Outlook.com

If you have an existing Microsoft e-mail account such as @hotmail, @MSN.com, or @Live.com, you can upgrade it to an Outlook.com account easily. Here's how:

1. **Log in to your existing account at Live.com.**

2. **Click or tap the Upgrade for Free link in the Outlook.com ad at the bottom right of your main page.**

   A screen appears explaining a bit about your new account with a video you can watch if you choose to.

3. **Click or tap the Continue to Inbox button, and you're done.**

If you later decide to switch back to your old Microsoft account, select the gear wheel icon in the upper-right of the page and choose Switch Back to Hotmail. You cannot switch back to an @MSN.com account; Microsoft is actively disabling the MSN.com domain.

Logging in to OneNote

As mentioned earlier in the chapter, logging in to OneNote allows you to customize your Office 2013 experience as well as sync settings across any device you use Office on. After you have a Microsoft account as described in the previous sections, follow these steps to log in:

1. **Open OneNote 2013.**

   A small window appears.

2. **Click or tap the Sign In button.**

3. **Enter the e-mail address and password for your Microsoft account and click Sign In.**

Click or tap your name in the upper-right corner of the OneNote window to find links to change your profile photo, account settings, and profile information.

Creating Notebooks, Sections, and Notes

To understand notes, you need to understand the basic organization of *notebooks,* which include *sections* and *pages* within those sections. The OneNote interface hails somewhat from Excel's multiple workbook tabs — the three or more tabs at the bottom of an Excel spreadsheet — except that in OneNote, each of those tabs would have an unlimited number of subtabs within it called *pages*.

Picture an actual notebook — not a cheapie knockoff with just paper in it, but an actual notebook with tabbed sections in it. As shown in Figure 1-1, you would write the title of the notebook on its cover, names of sections on the tabs interspersed between the pages, and then write your notes in the notebook on the actual pages between those section tabs. See Figure 1-2 to see what this translates to when looking at OneNote.

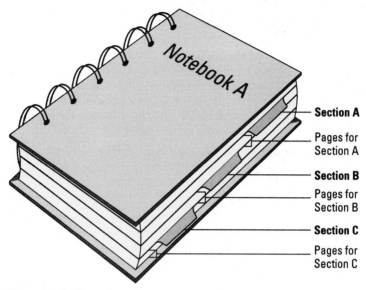

Figure 1-1: An illustration of pages within sections within notebooks.

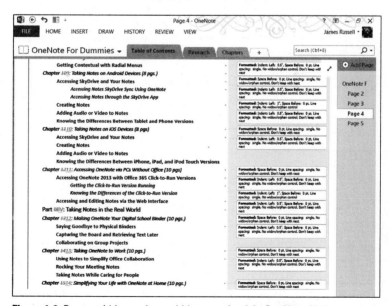

Figure 1-2: Pages within sections within a notebook in OneNote 2013.

As an example of how this structure can work for a notebook, I'll use a notebook I created for this book. I named the notebook (surprise!) *OneNote For Dummies*. Within this notebook I have the following sections — I can add more, but for illustration, I've kept it simple with three main sections:

✔ **Table of Contents:** Books begin as proposals, and one of the key pieces of a proposal is a proposed table of contents (TOC) that outlines the book's structure. In this section, I include the first proposed TOC on its own page as well as all major revisions of it on subsequent pages so that I can see the progression of the book's content as it's developed.

✔ **Research:** All research done for the book, including web pages, help documentation, and so forth go in separate pages in this section.

✔ **Chapters Completed:** In this section, I include a page with check boxes, one for each chapter by its number, so that I can check each off as I finish it and see at a glance how complete the book is at a given time. I include a separate page for each major process, including writing, technical editor revisions, copy edit revisions, and proofs.

Creating a notebook

You can create a notebook in OneNote easily; the process depends to some degree upon the destination folder or drive. Follow these steps to create a notebook:

1. **Open OneNote 2013, click or tap the File tab, and select New.**

   The New Notebook pane appears, as shown in Figure 1-3.

2. **Choose the place where you want to store the new notebook.**

   By default, you have SkyDrive and Computer as places. You can also add more SkyDrive accounts or Office 365 SharePoint accounts; see Chapter 2 for information on setting up a new place.

   If you choose SkyDrive but haven't signed in to SkyDrive yet, you'll have to click or tap the Sign In button and sign in with your Microsoft account.

3. **Type a name for the notebook in the Notebook Name field.**

   If you chose "Computer" for your place, the notebook opens, and you're done. If you chose another place, go to the next step.

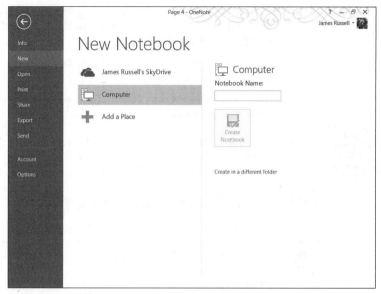

Figure 1-3: The New Notebook pane.

4. **Click or tap the Create Notebook button.**

   OneNote asks whether you want to share the notebook with other people; if so, click Invite People and see Chapter 10.

5. **Click or tap Not Now to create the new notebook.**

   The new notebook opens in the OneNote window.

Creating a new section

After you open a notebook, creating a section is simple; here's how:

1. **Open OneNote, click or tap File, and open the notebook you want to add a section to.**

2. **Click or tap the New Section tab to the right of the notebook's drop-down menu in the upper-left corner of the window (it's a blank tab with a + symbol on it).**

   A blank page appears below the section tab. At the right side of the window, you can see the page is titled Untitled Note.

3. **Click or tap the name on the tab — by default it's New Section #, where # is the number of the new section; for example, New Section 1.**

   The section's title is highlighted, indicating you can enter a new one to replace it.

4. **Enter the section's new title via physical or onscreen keyboard and press Enter.**

You can also right-click, or press and hold on a section tab, and choose New Section.

Creating a new section group

If you right-click or press and hold on a section **tab or on a** blank space on the section tab bar, you'll see a Create New Section Group item. Use this to create a totally new group of section tabs underneath the existing one. When in another section group, you'll see an up arrow to the right of the notebook name; click or tap that arrow to go up a level to the parent section group. Figure 1-4 shows a section group with the up button and a new section group being created.

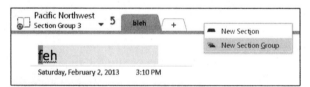

Figure 1-4: Creating a new section group.

Creating a new note page

When you create a new section, a new note page is automatically created, called simply Untitled Page. Follow these steps to add a new page:

1. **Open the notebook and section you want to add a new page to.**

2. **Click or tap the Add Page item in the sidebar at the right side of the OneNote window.**

3. **Right-click or press and hold on the page's name and choose Rename to rename the page; use the physical or onscreen keyboard to type.**

OneNote 2013 on Windows 7

Windows 7 is the oldest version of Windows that Office 2013 will run on. While OneNote 2013 works just fine on Windows 7, Office 2013 was designed at the same time as Windows 8 and was optimized for that system's more minimal interface. As a result, OneNote and other Office apps do look a bit funky on the Windows 7 interface, which still includes the Aero interface; Aero is Microsoft's name for the shiny, glasslike interface that began with Windows Vista and ended with Windows 7.

Saving Files . . . or Not

If you've used Office apps before other than OneNote — or, for that matter, any word processor, image-creation application, or spreadsheet application (among others) — you're probably used to having to save your files every so often by selecting File⇨Save or pressing Ctrl+S to ensure you don't lose your work.

Throw the concept of manually saving out of your head when thinking about OneNote; you won't see a Save option on the File tab, although you will see an Export option that lets you save a copy of the current notebook, section, or page under a different filename, in a different file format, or to a different place. See Chapter 2 for more info on exporting in OneNote 2013.

 OneNote calls saving *syncing* and does this automatically for you as you make changes as well as when you close OneNote.

Getting to Know the OneNote 2013 Interface

OneNote is an Office app, but, other than having the Ribbon, it doesn't resemble other apps in the suite very much. The following sections get you up to speed with the various pieces of the OneNote interface.

Identifying parts of the OneNote window

The OneNote interface is broken up into several major sections, as you can see from Figure 1-5, and as described in the following list:

✔ **Quick Launch bar:** A staple of Office suite apps, this bar comes by default with three command icons on it: a Back button that works much like a Back button on a web browser, Undo that lets you undo the last action, and Dock to Desktop that places the OneNote interface as a sidebar to the right side of your desktop.

✔ **Ribbon:** Office has had a Ribbon since the Office 2007 suite. The OneNote 2013 Ribbon has changed significantly in the latest version of the app, and I discuss it in the next section.

✔ **Notebook drop-down menu, section tabs, and Search bar:** Use these items to change notebooks, switch between sections, or search for content within your notebook.

✔ **Current Page pane:** This pane shows the page you're currently taking notes on.

✔ **Pages sidebar:** All pages within the current section are listed here with an Add Page link at the top. New pages are appended to the bottom of the list.

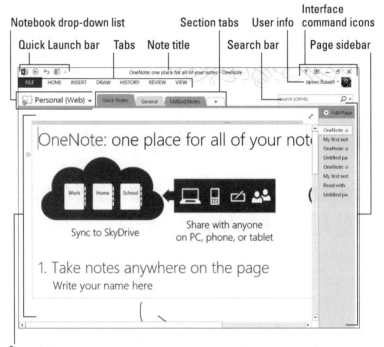

Figure 1-5: The different pieces of the OneNote interface.

Acquainting yourself with the revised Ribbon

The Office Ribbon was introduced in Office 2007 and was modified somewhat in Office 2010, mainly to replace the Office button with the File tab. The Office 2013 Ribbon has been modified in more dramatic fashion, not just visually but also to make it easier to use the suite on touchscreens. The following sections show you how the Ribbon is organized by tabs and gets you up to speed with what's different this time around.

Checking out the OneNote tabs

Later chapters discuss the actual tabs on the Ribbon in depth, but the default tabs are as follows:

- ✔ **File:** File-related options, as well as app options, are accessible here. This is where you share, export, and otherwise manage notebook files. See Chapter 2 for more info on the File tab.

- ✔ **Home:** Here you'll find the most-used options, including clipboard-centric options, the Format Painter, formatting options, and tabs. See Chapter 3 for more info on the Home tab.

- ✔ **Insert:** From this tab, you can insert non-OneNote objects into your notes. See Chapter 4 for more info on the Insert tab.

- ✔ **Draw:** Touchscreen-related options live here, including pens, highlighters, and other ink-related options. See the "Drawing in OneNote" section later in this chapter for more info on the Draw tab.

- ✔ **Review:** Options related to document review, such as tracking changes depending on who made them, are housed on this tab. See Chapter 10 for more info on the Review tab.

- ✔ **View:** Change the view of your notes on this tab. See Chapter 2 for more info on the View tab.

Seeing what has changed on the Ribbon

The Ribbon has changed a lot in OneNote 2013. Note the following new features of the OneNote Ribbon:

- ✔ **A more minimalist look:** Microsoft decided that the Office 2010 interface — and the Windows 7 interface, as well — were too shiny, colorful, and distracting. As a result, the Office 2013 Ribbon was redesigned to simplify icons, gray out options not currently usable, and remove color from all Ribbon tabs except for the File tab and the text of the currently selected tab.

✔ **More space between Ribbon command icons:** Although it was easy enough with a mouse cursor to pick out the correct icon on the Office 2010 Ribbon, using a touchscreen — and thus your fingertip — doesn't give you the precision that the tiny mouse cursor does. For this reason, command icons on the Ribbon are now farther apart than they were in earlier Office versions, making accessing them on a touchscreen much easier.

✔ **The Ribbon Display Options button:** Click or tap this button, which looks like an up arrow in a box, to access new options for the Ribbon, including the following:

- *Auto-hide Ribbon:* Just as Windows allows you to auto-hide the desktop taskbar and the Windows 8 charms are auto-hidden by default, OneNote and other Office apps now allow you to auto-hide the Ribbon so that you can click or tap the thin bar at the top of the screen to summon the Ribbon and then click or tap back into the document to make it go away.

- *Show Tabs:* Choose this to see only the Ribbon's tabs, increasing the size of the note-taking display significantly. To show a tab's Ribbon, click or tap it once; click or tap the tab again to hide the Ribbon.

- *Show Tabs and Commands:* This option — the default — shows the full Ribbon, with tabs and commands.

The Office Ribbon breaks up commands by category, grouping similarly themed items together in sections. The sections of the Home tab's Ribbon, along with summaries of the commands within each, are described in Chapter 3.

Drawing in OneNote

OneNote 2013 is the app Microsoft used to create and hone its digital pen technology, and when using OneNote with a pen device, you can truly get a lot more out of the app in terms of its writing and drawing capabilities than you can without one — writing and/ or drawing with a mouse is at best torture and at worst flat-out useless. Figure 1-6 shows how wretched writing looks when using a mouse.

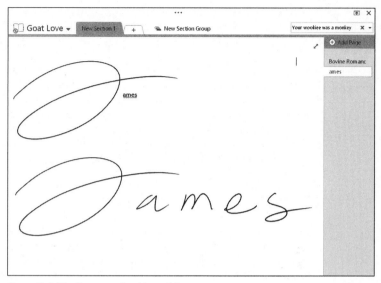

Figure 1-6: The horrors of writing with a mouse.

In the following sections I introduce you to drawing and writing in OneNote 2013 with a digital pen device. In Chapter 3, I show you how to turn handwriting into text.

If you're into self-mutilation and want to try writing or drawing with a mouse, the following sections will apply to you to various degrees, but you won't have the pressure-sensitivity that the digital pen gives you — your lines will be the same width and darkness no matter how you write on the screen.

Introducing the pen

The digital pen that comes with the Surface Pro looks a lot like a regular pen, but it is black, and its tip is a light blue color. Figure 1-7 shows an illustration of the pen just so I can point out the major features, which I discuss in later sections.

Figure 1-7: The various parts of the Surface Pro digital pen.

If you're left-handed, ambidextrous, or right-handed with a tablet set for left-handed use, you can change the "handedness" of your tablet in the Control Panel. The setting pretty much decides which side of your hand a menu will appear on: for righties, the menu will appear to the left of an item; for lefties, the menu will appear to the right of an item. To change the handedness of your tablet, simply access the Control Panel, select the Hardware and Sound category, access the Tablet PC Settings category, and then click or tap the Specify Which Hand You Write With link. You can then choose which hand you write with on the Other tab of the Tablet PC Settings window that appears and click or tap OK.

Navigating the Draw tab

The Draw tab in OneNote 2013 represents the digital ink technologies that truly come alive with the digital pen. Figure 1-8 shows the Draw tab, and the following list describes the various sections and commands on it.

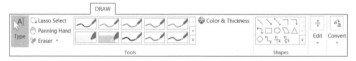

Figure 1-8: The OneNote 2013 Draw tab.

✔ **Tools:** This section includes all pen-and-ink-related items. On the left, you have various commands that change the way you work with items.

• **Type:** Allows you to work with your mouse and keyboard.

When you start freaking out about how to get your mouse cursor back, you want to click or tap this.

• **Lasso Select:** Lasso items with your cursor to convert them or move them as a group.

• **Panning Hand:** Click or tap and drag the page around without affecting the elements on it.

• **Erasers:** You have several sizes of erasers to choose from.

Use the Stroke Eraser to quickly delete entire strokes of ink rather than having to erase with an actual eraser.

• **Pens and Highlighters Box:** Here you'll see the built-in pens and highlighters; click one to select it or customize one, and it'll be added to your favorite pens automatically. At the bottom of the box, you'll see the Pen Mode drop-down menu that lets you switch between drawing only, handwriting only, or drawing and handwriting.

The Use Pen as Pointer option here allows you to *appear* to mark up the document, for example to circle an item to point it out to people in a sharing session, but the lines are not saved; they are merely indicatory.

- **Color & Thickness:** Choose a color for your custom pen or highlighter.

✔ **Shapes:** Choose from a number of shapes to draw onto your page. The Snap to Grid option forces shapes to snap to a grid if you're using gridlines on your page. The Lock Drawing Mode is present if you aren't using a pen device and helps you draw straight lines and shapes.

✔ **Edit:** Use these items to insert spacing, delete items, or arrange items by sending items in back of others or at the front of others, or to rotate items.

✔ **Convert:** Select the ink you want to change, and press one of the two buttons here to convert ink to text or math.

Chapter 2

Managing Notes and Configuring OneNote

• •

In This Chapter

▶ Putting your notes in order

▶ Saving your notes with sync

▶ Saving notes as other file types by exporting

▶ Configuring OneNote options

• •

*O*neNote is similar in many respects to other Office apps, but at the same time, the app is Microsoft's pet project for pushing the borders of Office and productivity apps in general. As I discuss in Chapter 1, the concept of saving files, for example, has changed dramatically. Additionally, as new as OneNote is in comparison to other apps, Microsoft was able to build it from the ground up without having to worry about legacy features or compatibility with other formats, such as Word needing to be compatible with WordPerfect, Apache OpenOffice, and other word-processing apps. The resulting OneNote interface is much simplified and intuitive, making it easy to make the app behave the way you want it to.

OneNote makes organizing your notes intuitive regardless of whether you store them on your device or in the cloud. In this chapter, I show you how to keep track of your notebooks, sections, and pages, including syncing, exporting, deleting, and changing their file type or location.

Rearranging Notes

Cutting, copying, and pasting files is a key skill to have when dealing with PCs or other devices in general, and with OneNote these processes allow you to easily rearrange and clean up notes.

Notebooks, by their nature, are the top level of notes, and thus you cannot make a copy of a notebook within OneNote itself; you can only cut, copy, and paste sections or pages from one notebook into another notebook. The only place you can make a copy of a notebook is within File Explorer (Windows Explorer in Windows 7 or prior versions) or SkyDrive.

Moving or copying sections or pages

If you find that a section or page either doesn't fit in its current notebook or section or would also fit in another notebook or section, you can easily move it from or copy it to the desired location. *Moving* a page results in the page disappearing from its original location; *copying* a page results in the page being present in both the original and target locations. The following sections show you how to move or copy a section or page.

Moving or copying a page

Moving or copying a page within its own section is as simple as dragging and dropping its item at the right side of the OneNote window to another location, but moving or copying a page to another section or notebook is a bit different. Follow these steps to do so:

1. **Right-click or press and hold on a page in the sidebar at the right side of the OneNote window, or Control-click multiple pages if using a keyboard, to move more than one page at a time; then choose Move or Copy.**

   The Move or Copy Pages window appears, as shown in Figure 2-1.

   You can also press Ctrl+Alt+M after selecting a page or pages to summon this window.

2. **Click or tap the + symbol next to a notebook's name and then select the section underneath it to choose the section you want to copy or move the page or pages to.**

3. **Click or tap either the Move or Copy button.**

   If you're moving a page, the page will disappear from the current section, and you'll have to visit the new location to find it; if you're copying a page, it will remain where it is and also be available in the notebook section you chose to copy it to.

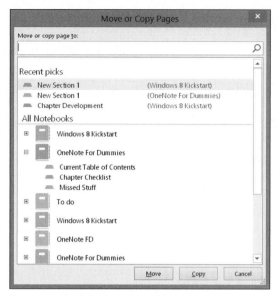

Figure 2-1: The Move or Copy Pages window.

Moving or copying a section

Just as with pages, you can always move a section within its notebook by simply dragging and dropping it before or after other section tabs, but moving or copying a section to another notebook is a different process. Follow these steps to do so:

1. **Right-click or press and hold on a section tab and choose Move or Copy.**

   The Move or Copy Section window appears; it looks nearly identical to the window in Figure 2-1, aside from the title bar.

2. **Click or tap the name of the notebook you want to move or copy the section to.**

   Click or tap the + symbol next to a notebook's name and then select a section underneath it to place the new section after the selected one. If you don't do so, the section will be placed after all existing sections in the notebook.

3. **Click or tap either the Move or Copy button.**

   If you're moving a section, it will disappear from the current notebook, and you'll have to visit the new location to find it; if you're copying a section, it will remain where it is and also be available in the notebook you chose to copy it to.

Merging sections

1. **Right-click or press and hold on a section tab and choose Merge into Another Section.**

   The Merge Section window appears; it looks nearly identical to Figure 2-1, except for the title bar and the Merge button.

2. **Click or tap the name of the notebook you want to move or copy the section to.**

3. **Click or tap the + symbol next to a notebook's name, select the section underneath it that you want to merge the current section with, and click or tap Merge.**

   The section disappears from the current notebook; access the section you chose to merge it with to find it.

Renaming Notes

Renaming notebooks, sections, and pages are different processes, with the renaming of notebooks by far being the most unintuitive. Here's how:

- ✔ **Rename notebooks' display names.** To rename a notebook's display name in OneNote, right-click or press and hold on the notebook's name in the upper left of the OneNote 2013 window, choose Properties, type a new name into the Display Name field, and click OK. This only affects the notebook's display name in OneNote, not the name of the folder.

  You can change the location of a notebook using the Change Location button on this window. This is also where you can change the format of the note to the 2007 format.

- ✔ **Rename notebook folders.** If you want to rename a notebook's folder, you have to do so within File Explorer or Windows Explorer. To do so, close OneNote, navigate to the OneNote Notebooks folder in your Documents folder, click or press and hold on the folder of the notebook so that the name becomes highlighted, and overtype the old name with the new one. Then restart OneNote and open the notebook using the File tab's Open command.

- ✔ **Rename sections or pages.** To rename a section or page, right-click or press and hold on the section tab or page item and overtype the existing name; then press Enter. For a page, you can also replace the name by clicking or tapping into the page and typing a new title in the title space at the top of the window.

Deleting Notes or Sections

Deleting notebooks, sections, or pages are different processes, and with notebooks, deleting them depends on whether you've saved your files to SkyDrive or to your computer. The following list describes how to delete all of these things.

✔ **Delete notebooks on your computer.** Deleting notebooks is not intuitive in OneNote at all, because it's not an action even represented on the OneNote 2013 interface. To delete a notebook, you have to delete the folder for it in Windows Explorer and delete the backup for it there as well. On my Windows 8 computer, the backup folder is at C:\Users\James\AppData\ Local\Microsoft\OneNote\15.0\Backup. Check the Save & Backup item in OneNote options to change backup options.

Note that you have to have hidden folders viewable (you can change this in File Explorer's Folder Options) to view the AppData folder or anything within it.

✔ **Delete notebooks on SkyDrive.** Simply log in to your SkyDrive, right-click or press and hold on the notebook, and choose Delete. The file will go to the SkyDrive Recycle Bin and will be deleted after 30 days.

✔ **Delete sections.** To delete a section, right-click or press and hold on its tab, and choose Delete. The section will go to the notebook's Recycle Bin, which is discussed in the next section.

✔ **Delete note pages.** Delete a page by right-clicking or pressing and holding on its name in the pages pane at the right side of the OneNote 2013 interface and choosing Delete. The page will go to the notebook's Recycle Bin, which is discussed in the next section.

Retrieving Deleted Notes

Deleted sections and note pages go to the Recycle Bin for that particular notebook, which you can access on the History tab. Files are expunged after 60 days, so you have until then to restore them. To restore a section or page, right-click it and use one of the Move, Merge, or Copy items to move it out of the Recycle Bin.

Each notebook has its own Recycle Bin, so if you're not seeing the item you're looking for, make sure you're in the correct notebook.

Viewing Unfiled Notes

When creating notes from a mobile device such as an Android smartphone, the new page will go into Unfiled Notes, which is a section in your Personal (Web) notebook. Visit that section to find those notes.

Syncing Notes

As mentioned briefly in Chapter 1, OneNote distances itself from the whole concept of manually saving files in favor of *syncing* them. The following sections describe how to sync files either automatically or manually.

Syncing automatically

OneNote auto-saves your notes every time you make any change at all to a notebook, section, or page; it also syncs when you close a file or the OneNote app.

OneNote can sync data to notes saved to SkyDrive, other networks, or other cloud services while you have an active connection to the Internet or the network the note is stored on. If the proper connection isn't present, OneNote keeps track of the changes internally and syncs when the connection is reestablished.

Syncing manually once

Although by default OneNote syncs notebooks not stored on your local device automatically, you can sync them manually at any time or configure the app to not sync automatically at all so that you have no choice but to sync manually.

To sync manually once, you have one of three options:

✔ Right-click or press and hold on the tab for the notebook and choose the Sync This Notebook Now option.

While the notebook is syncing, if you decide to cancel the sync, click or tap the Cancel Sync button. You'll have to be quick, though; as with a broadband Internet connection, the sync process is pretty fast.

✔ Open the Shared Notebook Synchronization window as described in the next section and click or tap the Sync All button to sync all notebooks.

✔ Open the Shared Notebook Synchronization window as described in the next section and click or tap the Sync Now button next to the notebook you want to sync.

Configuring manual sync

You may have any number of reasons to not want OneNote to sync your notes manually — for example, if you're collaborating on a project and don't want your colleagues to see your changes until they're 100 percent done.

Follow these steps to configure OneNote so that it will not sync automatically:

1. **Right-click or press and hold on the notebook name in the upper-left corner of the OneNote window and choose Notebook Sync Status.**

   The Shared Notebook Synchronization window appears, as shown in Figure 2-2.

   Only notebooks saved to SkyDrive or another remote location are listed.

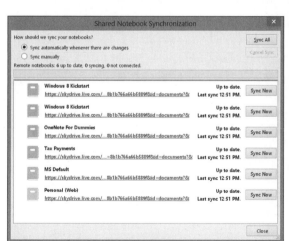

Figure 2-2: The Shared Notebook Synchronization window.

2. **Select the Sync Manually radio button at the top of the page.**

3. **Click or tap the Close button.**

Exporting Notes

The command known as Save As in other apps allows you to save a file under a different name or location; this process is called *export* in OneNote. The following sections show you how to export a notebook, section, or page.

1. **Click or tap the File tab and select Export.**

   The Export Current pane appears at right, as shown in Figure 2-3.

   If using a keyboard and mouse, you can Ctrl+click multiple pages to export multiple pages in the same file.

2. **Select Page, Section, or Notebook, choose the format you want for exporting, and click or tap the Export button.**

   The Save As window appears, indicating that the concept of saving versus exporting hasn't quite made it to all interface elements yet.

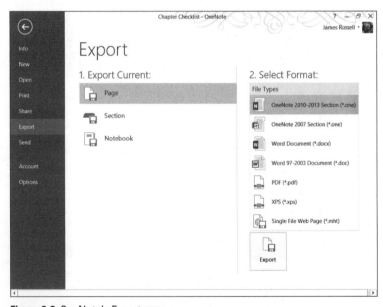

Figure 2-3: OneNote's Export pane.

When exporting a whole notebook, you have three choices for the format you want to export to:

- **OneNote package file:** This format uses the `.onepkg` file extension.

- **Portable Document Format:** This ubiquitous format uses the `.pdf` extension and is compatible with any device that supports PDF, which includes, by far, most devices.

- **XML Paper Specification:** Microsoft designed the XPS format, which is similar to PDF in terms of usability but is compiled using XML. This format is compatible with Microsoft Reader in Windows 8 and the Microsoft XPS Document Writer that you see in Print dialog boxes throughout Windows 7 and Windows 8.

When exporting a section or page, you also have the following choices:

- **OneNote 2010–2013 Section:** Using the `.one` file extension, this format is the latest version of the OneNote file format.

- **OneNote 2007 Section:** While this format also uses the `.one` extension, it supports a more limited feature set than the OneNote 2010–2013 format.

- **Word Document:** Supporting the Word format used in 2007–2013, this format uses the `.docx` format.

- **Word 97–2003 Document:** This older format, utilizing the `.doc` extension, supports older versions of Word.

- **Single File Web Page:** This format uses the MIME HTML document format `.mht` (abbreviated version of `.mhtml`), which saves an entire web page in a single file.

If you chose, for example, to save the current notebook and realize as the Save As window appears that you want to save the currently selected section or pages instead, you can do so from the appropriate radio button in the Page Range section below the Save As Type drop-down list.

3. **Click or tap Save to export the file.**

Configuring OneNote

As with other Office apps, you can configure OneNote to your tastes with ease. You can customize the appearance of the Ribbon, as I discuss in Chapter 1, and change the buttons on the Quick Launch bar, pin or unpin panes, and more. The following sections show you how.

Changing account settings

If you've logged in to OneNote with a Microsoft account as described in Chapter 1, you have settings you can configure at will to personalize your OneNote experience. To view your account, do one of the following:

- ✔ Click or tap your account name in the upper-right corner of the window and choose Account Settings.

- ✔ Click or tap the File tab and select Account.

Regardless of which way you choose to access your account options, the Account pane appears, as shown in Figure 2-4.

From the Account pane you can change the following settings:

- ✔ **User Information:** This section includes links to customize user data. The first two links bring up your profile at Live. com where you can change your photo, contact information, and profile information. The second two links allow you to sign out of OneNote or switch accounts.

- ✔ **Office Background:** The drop-down list under this heading includes quite a few Ribbon backgrounds from which you can choose; Figure 2-4 shows the Underwater background.

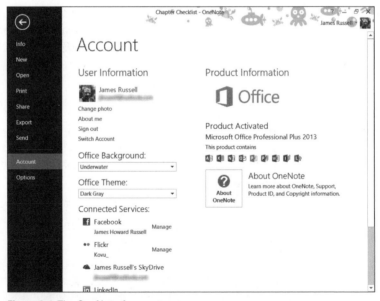

Figure 2-4: The OneNote Account pane.

- ✔ **Office Theme:** Choose here from one of three color themes: White, Light Gray, and Dark Gray. The Dark Gray theme eliminates the purple color of OneNote altogether, whereas the Light Gray theme just darkens it. Figure 2-4 shows the Dark Gray theme.

- ✔ **Connected Services:** This section shows all external services you have associated with your Microsoft account, whether or not they're useful for OneNote. For example, there's no Facebook integration in OneNote, but the associated Facebook service is still listed here. To add a service, click or tap the Add Service button and choose the service to add. You'll have to log in to the service using your account name and password.

- ✔ **Product Information:** Look in this section to see the version of Office you have, icons representing the apps included in it, whether the product is activated, and the About OneNote button that shows you more information.

Customizing the Quick Launch bar

The Quick Launch bar is at the top left of the OneNote window and includes icons representing shortcuts to often-used commands.

Click or tap the tiny down-pointing arrow to the right of these icons to add or remove icon commands. To add a list item to the Quick Launch bar, click or tap it, which places a check mark next to it; do the same to remove the check mark and thus remove the icon from the bar. By default, the bar includes, from left to right, the Back, Undo, and Dock to Desktop commands.

The icons on the menu represent the most popular choices, as follows:

- ✔ **Back:** This icon operates exactly like a web browser's Back button, taking you to the last page you were looking at.

- ✔ **Forward:** Like a web browser's Forward button, this button takes you to the last page from which you used the Back button.

- ✔ **Undo:** Use this command too undo the last performed action.

- ✔ **Redo:** Click or tap this icon to redo the last action you undid.

- ✔ **Print:** This icon takes you to the OneNote Print window where you can set up your printout and choose where to print.

- ✔ **Print Preview:** Use this button to preview your printout.

- ✔ **Dock to Desktop:** Use this command to place the OneNote window in a narrow strip at the side of your desktop.

✔ **Favorite Pen 1–4:** If you use OneNote's drawing tools as I describe in Chapter 1, you can define multiple favorite pens and use these items for easy access to them.

✔ **Favorite Highlighter 1:** Similar to the Favorite Pen items, this button accesses your favorite highlighter.

✔ **Touch/Mouse Mode:** This icon toggles between touch and mouse mode; the former puts more space between commands on the Ribbon to make them easier to access with a fingertip.

The bottom two items on the list are the More Commands item and the Show Quick Access Toolbar Below the Ribbon item. Select the former to open the Quick Access Toolbar section of the OneNote Options window, as discussed in the next section; select the latter to place the Quick Access bar below the Ribbon.

Navigating OneNote's options

OneNote 2013 includes options similar to other Office apps as well as options that are all its own. You can view OneNote's options by clicking or tapping on the File tab and choosing Options.

Mouse over or press on the little *i* with a circle around it at the right side of any option to see more information about it.

✔ **General:** The options in this section allow you to customize how OneNote works in general, including the following:

- Choose whether you want the Mini Toolbar to appear when you select text to give you access to common formatting options

- Set the default font and font color

- Personalize your name, initials, Office background and theme, and instruct the app to use that information regardless of which account you're signed in with for consistency in tracking your changes to documents

✔ **Display:** A rather slim list of options, these settings allow you to change the look of OneNote (although, weirdly, the background and theme are listed on the General tab). Choose from such options as how new pages look, Quick Note docking options, and where tabs, scroll bars, and navigation and notification bars appear.

✔ **Proofing:** These options change how OneNote corrects and highlights errors in your text. For example, you can configure the app to ignore uppercase words, ignore Internet and file addresses, flag repeated words, and use custom dictionaries. You can also decide whether to allow OneNote to check spelling or grammar and customize how the app handles French and Spanish text. The AutoCorrect Options button, located at the top of the window, summons the window of the same name. Click or tap the button to summon the window, as shown in Figure 2-5.

As you can see from the figure, you can add Replace shortcuts in addition to configuring how and whether OneNote autocorrects certain things; you can use the Exceptions button if you want to keep the setting active but create exceptions for it to ignore, and you can choose the Math AutoCorrect tab to customize how the app replaces text shortcuts with mathematical symbols.

✔ **Save & Backup:** This section, shown in Figure 2-6, lets you modify the default save locations and intervals of saved and backed up notes, as well as the default location for cache files. Also here are buttons allowing you to back up notebooks or changed files along with options to configure file optimization.

✔ **Send to OneNote:** Here you can configure where you want content from other apps, such as Outlook 2013, web browsers, or screen clippings, to land in OneNote. By default, all items say Always Ask Where to Send, but you can change this setting to the current page or a new page, or you can set a certain location for the content.

Figure 2-5: The AutoCorrect window.

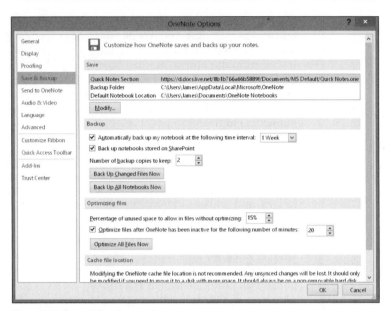

Figure 2-6: Save & Backup options.

✔ **Audio & Video:** Set the audio recording and video recording settings here, such as devices, input, codec, format, and profile.

Check the check box at the bottom to allow searching of audio and video recordings for certain words, making OneNote's search capabilities even more powerful.

✔ **Language:** If you have multiple languages installed for Office, use the options on this pane to customize which languages are used and when. For example, if your native language is different from the language you're writing in, you can set the tooltip and help languages to be different from the display language.

✔ **Advanced:** This section is pretty big, and describing each of the options would take up a chapter in itself; however, briefly, with these options you can configure advanced options for editing; linked notes; pen inking (see Chapter 1), e-mail sent from OneNote; optimizing battery use; configuring tag and password options; choosing whether to insert long printouts on one or multiple pages; disabling hardware graphics acceleration or text recognition in pictures; and changing measurement units.

✔ **Customize Ribbon:** Shown in Figure 2-7, this is the most complex item of the lot. Essentially, your existing tabs are shown in a pane on the right by default, and the list of available commands appears on the left. By default, the left pane lists popular commands, and the right pane lists your main tabs, but you can change the left pane to list all commands, commands not on the Ribbon, or commands on various tabs. Simply select the command you want to add to the pane on the right and click or tap the Add button between panes to add it; to remove a command, select it in the right pane and then click or tap the Remove button.

The pane on the right can be changed to All Tabs, Main Tabs, or Tool Tabs for processes such as playback, table, and equation tools. Use the buttons at the bottom right of the window to create tabs and groups of commands on tabs and to rename tabs, reset customizations, or import or export them.

✔ **Quick Access Toolbar:** Similar to the Customize Ribbon tab, the Quick Access Toolbar options allow you to add or remove commands to or from the toolbar. On the left is the pane including commands you can add, and on the right is a pane showing what's currently on the toolbar. Select the command you want to add to the pane on the right and click or tap the Add button between panes to add it; to remove a command, select it in the right pane and then click or tap the Remove button.

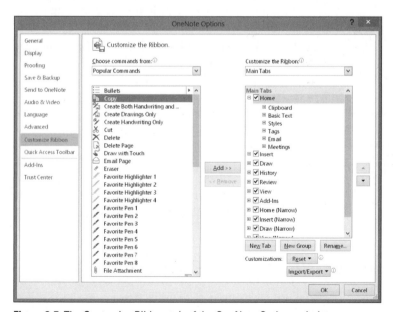

Figure 2-7: The Customize Ribbon tab of the OneNote Options window.

You can also access the Quick Access Toolbar options by selecting the More Options button on the menu accessible via the little black downward-pointing arrow to the right of the icons on the Quick Access toolbar.

✔ **Add-Ins:** COM — or Component Object Model — add-ins are created by third parties to extend the capabilities of OneNote. The only two items in the drop-down list on this pane include COM Add-Ins and Disabled Items.

✔ **Trust Center:** The Trust Center allows you to configure security for OneNote.

Configuring View options

The OneNote 2013 View tab, shown in Figure 2-8, allows you to change the way your notes look and how OneNote looks and behaves. The following groups of commands are available to you on the View tab:

✔ **Views:** Choose from these commands to toggle between Normal view, Full-page view, and to dock OneNote to the desktop.

✔ **Page Setup:** Choose from these options to change the color of the page, add rules or gridlines, hide the page title, or change the size of the paper.

✔ **Zoom:** These items let you decide on the zoom level of the page and change the page width.

✔ **Window:** Summon a new window, new docked window, open the Send to OneNote tool, or make OneNote always appear on top of other windows.

Figure 2-8: OneNote 2013's View tab.

Password-Protecting Sections

If you use OneNote to take notes that you want to keep private, securing individual notes is as simple as password-protecting sections. The following sections show you how to add or remove a password from a section.

Oddly, you cannot password-protect entire notebooks, but securing individual sections — and thus the pages within — amounts to the same thing, except that someone could at least see the names of the sections.

Adding a password to a section

Adding a password to a section is a quick process. Here's how:

1. **Select the Review tab in OneNote and click or tap the Password button.**

   The Password Protection pane appears at the right side of the window, as shown in Figure 2-9.

2. **Select the Set Password button.**

   The Password Protection window appears.

3. **Enter a password in the two fields on the Password Protection window and click or tap OK.**

    A pop-up window appears asking if you want to keep or delete existing backups of the section that do not have the password. If you choose to delete the existing backups, future backups will be password-protected just like the original.

   Make sure you keep your password written down or somewhere else; if you lose it, you will also lose your data.

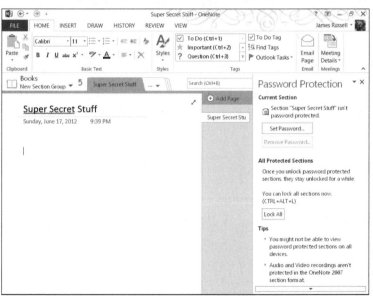

Figure 2-9: The Password Protection pane.

Pass phrases are better than passwords

A *pass phrase* is much harder to crack than a regular password and consists of four random words strung together, such as *catcrackrockfiend.* Microsoft allows you to use up to 16 characters for a password (all characters after the sixteenth one are ignored). For even more security, substitute symbols or numbers for at least a few of the characters and make one or more of the letters uppercase, such as *C@tcrackr0ckF13nd.*

Removing a password from a section

You can remove a password from a section easily as long as you have the section's password. To remove the password protection from a section, follow these steps:

1. **Select the Review tab in OneNote and click or tap the Password button.**

   The Password Protection pane appears at the right side of the window.

2. **Select the Remove Password button.**

   The Remove Password window appears with a single field.

3. **Enter the correct password in the field and click or tap OK.**

Chapter 3

Formatting Notes

· ·

· ·

*T*aking notes with OneNote is intuitive and even fun after you get used to the basics. As an Office app, of course, OneNote has formatting options, but beyond simple formatting, using tags allows you to label and organize each piece of content in a note by type so that you can easily find content you're looking for later. You can also add images and audio to your notes, extract text from images, and translate handwritten ink notes into text you can work with and format.

In this chapter, I introduce you to these features and more.

Formatting Notes

Some OneNote formatting controls show up in other Office apps, most notably Microsoft Word, but there are many formatting options exclusive to OneNote. The following sections discuss the basic formatting options on the OneNote 2013 Ribbon as well as OneNote tags, which help you organize note content easily.

Checking out the standard Office formatting tools

If you've used Microsoft Word at all, the first three sections of the OneNote Home tabs, shown in Figure 3-1, will look pretty familiar, if a bit sparse in comparison to Word. From left to right, these sections are

- **Clipboard:** Options in this section relate to the Windows Clipboard. Paste is by far the largest button. The small arrow at the bottom of the Paste button allows you to keep the original formatting of the text, to merge formatting from the original text with the new, or to keep only the pasted text and none of the formatting at all. Rounding out the options in this section are Cut and Copy and, of course, the venerable Format Painter.

  While on a paragraph or line that you want to copy the formatting from, click or tap the Format Painter icon; then select another paragraph to apply the formatting to that second line that you want to format. To apply the copied formatting to multiple items, double-click or double-tap the Format Painter; double-click or double-tap the Format Painter to *forget* the current formatting when you're done.

- **Basic Text:** These items should be pretty familiar; they're not only in Microsoft Word but also in many applications that allow text formatting, such as WordPad. The top row includes font, font size, bullets, and numbered list options as well as a Clear Formatting item; the bottom row includes standard text format options such as bold, italic, underscore, highlighting, text color, justification options, line spacing, and table border options.

- **Styles:** Styles are basically groups of text formats saved into one style so that you can apply all of that formatting to a paragraph with one click rather than adding each font option manually. Available styles include six levels of headings as well as styles for quotes, code, citations, and page titles. The Normal style is the default style for all OneNote text.

  Unlike other Office apps, OneNote has a limited set of styles because it isn't a word processor. If you want to create styles, do so in Word and then copy and paste the paragraphs into OneNote. OneNote will accept the formatting but will not import the style into OneNote — you can't create or import styles in OneNote like you can in Word. If you want to use the same formatting, you'll have to use Format Painter or just re-create the formatting manually.

- **Tags:** Tags allow you to highlight and organize information in notes. See the next section for more information on tags.

- **E-mail:** Select the E-mail Page item — the only item on the E-mail button — to e-mail the note to someone using Microsoft Outlook.

  This item will fail if you select it before you've set up Outlook 2013.

Figure 3-1: The Home tab Ribbon.

Highlight note content with tags

The fourth section on the Home tab of OneNote's Ribbon is exclusive to OneNote: tags. OneNote tags allow you to format individual parts of notes for easy searches, quick access, and easy organization. Need to follow up with your manager? Tag the item as such. Need to add contact info for a colleague or client? Tag it. The following list describes the many items available to you in this section.

Checking out the default tags

Microsoft has populated OneNote with a well-rounded set of standard tags that are good for business, home, or school use. The first nine items on the Tags drop-down list, shown in Figure 3-2, can be accessed by pressing the Ctrl key and a number, as indicated in the following list.

✔ **To Do (Ctrl+1):** This item places an empty check box to the left of the item so that, when you accomplish the task, you can click or tap to check the item, indicating completion.

✔ **Important (Ctrl+2):** Select this item to place a yellow star to the left of the item.

Figure 3-2: The Tags drop-down list.

✔ **Question (Ctrl+3):** Use this tag to mark questions you need answers to. A purple question mark appears to the left of the item.

✔ **Remember for Later (Ctrl+4):** Remind yourself to review an item in the future. The item is highlighted in yellow.

✔ **Definition (Ctrl+5):** Use this item to call out a definition in green highlighting.

✔ **Highlight (Ctrl+6):** Dubiously useful, this tag places a small icon of a highlighter pen to the left of the item. You can use this icon any time you use a highlighter so that you can search for highlighted items later.

✔ **Contact (Ctrl+7):** Choose this tag to place a little contact icon that resembles a contact card to the left of the item.

✔ **Address (Ctrl+8):** Add a little house icon to the left of the item to indicate that it's an address.

✔ **Phone Number (Ctrl+9):** Mark the item as a phone number with an old-style phone-handset icon to the left of the item. Figure 3-3 shows several note items formatted as phone number, address, and contact.

⊞ James H. Russell
☎ 555-555-5555
⌂ Grover Beach, CA 93433

Figure 3-3: A phone number, address, and contact.

✔ **Website to Visit:** Indicate a page you need to visit later with a globe icon with a symbol representing a hyperlink below it.

✔ **Idea:** Add a light-bulb icon to an item to indicate that you just had a stroke of genius . . . or at least a great idea.

✔ **Password:** Utilize this tag to indicate either that a password is required for the item or that the item is, in fact, a password.

Keeping important passwords in written or electronic form is a bad idea for security, but if you have to do so, ensure the security of your note and, if you're using it, SkyDrive. See Chapter 5 for more info on SkyDrive.

✔ **Critical:** Use this tag for super-important items that need to be resolved immediately.

✔ **Project A and Project B:** Choose either of these to indicate that an item belongs to a certain project. The default icons for these two tags are a red and yellow box, respectively. Whether you decide to make Project A dependent upon or independent from Project B is entirely up to you: It's your note.

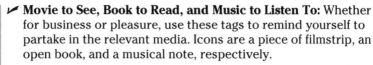 ✔ **Movie to See, Book to Read, and Music to Listen To:** Whether for business or pleasure, use these tags to remind yourself to partake in the relevant media. Icons are a piece of filmstrip, an open book, and a musical note, respectively.

 ✔ **Source for Article:** Mark a source for an article you're writing with this tag; note that the icon for this tag is identical to the Website to Visit tag: a globe icon with a hyperlink symbol below it.

 ✔ **Remember for Blog:** Use this tag to mark items you want to post about on your blog. The icon looks like a text bubble.

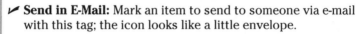 ✔ **Discuss with [Person A, Person B, Manager]:** These three tags flag the need to discuss specific items with other people. Whom you designate as Person A, Person B, or Manager is up to you.

 The icons for all three look the same, except that the Discuss with Manager icon is orange instead of blue.

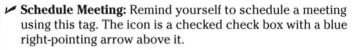 ✔ **Send in E-Mail:** Mark an item to send to someone via e-mail with this tag; the icon looks like a little envelope.

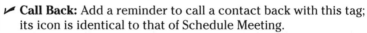 ✔ **Schedule Meeting:** Remind yourself to schedule a meeting using this tag. The icon is a checked check box with a blue right-pointing arrow above it.

 ✔ **Call Back:** Add a reminder to call a contact back with this tag; its icon is identical to that of Schedule Meeting.

 ✔ **To Do Priority:** Two priorities exist here by default: 1 and 2. Priority 1 items have an icon with a "1" against a blue background; Priority 2 items have an icon with a white "2" against an orange background. You can customize these icons or create more of them; see later sections in the chapter for more information on adding, modifying, and customizing tags.

 ✔ **Client Request:** Use this tag to call out items that were requested by a client; the icon is a yellow exclamation mark next to a checked check box.

Adding tags to note content

To add a tag, simply select the note content that you want to add a tag to, choose the tag from the Tags drop-down list, or use the keyboard shortcut for the tag if it has one. The tag's icon will appear to the left of the item.

Searching for tags

The main purpose for tags is to organize note content for easy access later. To find a tag or tags, follow these steps:

1. **Select the Home tab on the Ribbon and click or tap Find Tags.**

   The Tags Summary pane appears at the right of the OneNote interface, as shown in Figure 3-4.

2. **Choose an item from the Group Tags By drop-down list box, depending on your preferences for sorting tags. The options on the list box include:**

   - **Tag Name:** List tags by name.

   - **Section:** List tags according to the section they're in.

   - **Title:** List tags according to title.

   - **Date:** List tags by date modified.

   - **Note Text:** Sort alphabetically by text accompanying the note.

3. **Click or tap a tag in the search results to navigate to that tag.**

Modifying tags

You can customize the names, icons, and so on for existing tags. Changes made to a tag are permanent but will not affect any uses of the tag prior to the change. For example, if you use the tag To Do with a check box as it is by default and change the icon later to a car icon, all To Do tags already in existence will still use the check box. To modify a tag, follow these steps:

1. **Right-click or press and hold on a tag in the drop-down list where all the tags are shown and choose Modify This Tag from the context menu that appears.**

   If you simply want to delete the tag, choose Delete This Tag from the menu.

   The Modify Tag dialog box appears, as shown in Figure 3-5. You can see a preview of what your tag will look like in the Preview pane.

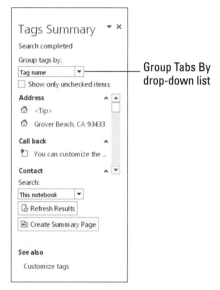

Group Tabs By
drop-down list

Figure 3-4: The OneNote Tags Summary pane.

Figure 3-5: The Modify Tag dialog box.

2. **Enter a new name in the Display Name field if desired. If you want, you can choose a new icon for the tag from the Symbol drop-down list, shown in Figure 3-6, as well as Font Color or Highlight Color from the appropriate drop-down lists.**

3. **Click or tap OK.**

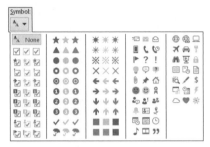

Figure 3-6: The Symbol drop-down list.

Customizing or creating tags

The Customize Tags option has two main purposes: It allows you to add tags, and it serves as a jumping-off point to modify tags (as discussed in the previous section). For example, perhaps you want to add a tag beyond the two default tags for projects: Project A and Project B. With the Customize Tags option, you can create another tag for Project C.

To modify a tag, right-click or press and hold on any tag and choose Customize Tags from the context menu that appears; from the Customize Tags window, select the tag and then click or tap Modify Tag and then follow Steps 2 and 3 in the previous section.

To create a new tag, follow these steps:

1. **Right-click or press and hold on any tag and choose Customize Tags from the context menu that appears.**

   The Customize Tags window appears, as shown in Figure 3-7.

Figure 3-7: The Customize Tags window.

By default, new tags are added to the top of the drop-down list, *but* the Ctrl keyboard shortcuts stay the same. So, if you add an icon and let it take the top spot, it takes on the Ctrl+1 keyboard shortcut, and all other tags get bumped down by one; the tag that had Ctrl+2 now has Ctrl+3, the tag that had Ctrl+9 has no tag, and so forth. Use the arrows at the upper right of this window to move tags up or down according to which shortcut you want them to have.

2. **Click or tap the New Tag button.**

3. **Choose a new icon for the tag from the Symbol drop-down list, shown in Figure 3-6, as well as Font Color or Highlight Color from the appropriate drop-down lists, as desired.**

Microsoft provides default symbols for you to choose from when you access the drop-down Symbols list box (refer to Figure 3-6). As you can see at the lower left of the figure, there are even nine symbols that you can use to create more To Do or Priority tags, with varying colors and the number 1-3 on them.

4. **Click or tap OK.**

Adding and Manipulating Images

Images can be a critical part of your notes, and OneNote gives you multiple methods of adding images to notes. Whether you want to paste an image in from your Clipboard or add an image from a folder on your computer, OneNote has got you covered. The following sections describe the various methods of adding images to your OneNote documents.

Adding images by copying and pasting

You can copy images from any web page by right-clicking or pressing and holding on an image and choosing Copy Image or a similar command from your browser's context menu to copy the image to your Windows Clipboard. Then you just paste the image into another application and save the image in a place where you can find it.

In addition to using your browser to copy images, you can capture your whole screen or individual windows to the Windows Clipboard — such as your author did to capture screenshots for this book — using the PrtSc/SysRq key. You can then paste the image into Microsoft Paint or other document-editing software and save it normally.

Once an image is copied to your Clipboard, pasting an image into OneNote is easy: Simply click in the document where you want the image and then do one of the following to paste the image on your Windows Clipboard into the current OneNote page:

✔ Press Ctrl+V.

✔ Right-click or press and hold on the place in the document where you want the image and then choose Paste.

Adding images by inserting

OneNote allows you to insert images from a folder on your computer as well as from a few other sources, including Microsoft's voluminous online clip art repository, a Bing Image Search, or your Flickr or SkyDrive account. Follow these steps to insert an image using the Insert tab, shown in Figure 3-8, on the Ribbon:

1. **With a document open, select the Insert tab on the Ribbon and then select either Pictures or Online Pictures in the Images section.**

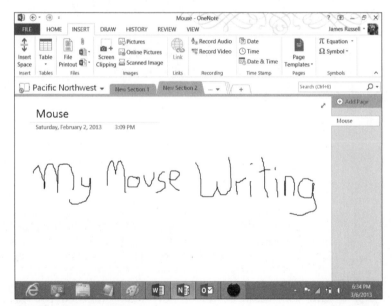

Figure 3-8: OneNote 2013's Insert tab.

2. If you chose Pictures, on your hard drive, navigate to the photo that you want to add and then click or tap Insert. If you chose Online Pictures, choose the service you want to add from, find and select an image, and choose Insert.

3. In the case of clip art or a Bing Image Search, enter a search term, select the Search button (it looks like a magnifying glass), choose the image, and then select Insert.

Adding images via the Screen Clipping tool

The Screen Clipping tool in OneNote 2013 has been dramatically improved. See Chapter 4 for info on using the Screen Clipping Tool to add images to your notes.

Retrieve text from images

OneNote has object content recognition (OCR) capabilities built into it, which allows you to retrieve text from images with just a few clicks or taps. Follow these steps to retrieve text from an image:

1. Insert an image into your note as described in the previous sections.

2. Right-click or press and hold on the image and choose Copy Text from Picture.

3. Paste the text from the image into a new note or other document so that you can edit and format it as desired.

OneNote will retrieve *all* text from the image. So that you don't wind up with text from the interface that you don't need, do yourself a favor and crop your image to just the text you want to retrieve using Paint or another graphics application.

Adding Audio and Video to Notes

OneNote allows you to record on the fly and add audio and video clips to your notes right from the OneNote Ribbon. You can also embed prerecorded clips by using the Ribbon's Insert tab. The following sections show you how to perform both functions.

Embedding an existing clip in your note

You can embed an audio or video clip into your note as a file attachment so that people can double-click or double-tap the icon for the file to view or listen to it. To embed an existing clip to your note, follow these steps:

1. **Open a page in your notebook section and position your cursor where you want the embedded file's icon to appear.**

2. **Select the Insert tab from the OneNote Ribbon and click or tap the File Attachment button with the paperclip icon on it.**

3. **Browse to the location of the clip, select it, and click or tap Insert.**

Recording a new clip to add to your note

No matter where you and your PC are, you can record audio or video to add to your notes. This can be useful in anywhere something is happening that you want to record and keep in a note. The process for recording a video and audio clip is the same except for the button you press to start the recording. Here's how:

1. **Open a page in your notebook section and position your cursor where you want the recorded file's icon to appear.**

2. **Select the Insert tab on the Ribbon and click or tap Record Audio or Record Video.**

   The clip begins recording. For a video, you'll see the video appear in a small window. Notice that the Ribbon adds an Audio/Video tab that includes recording and playback controls.

3. **Click or tap the Stop button with a big square on it to stop recording.**

4. **Hover your mouse over the clip's icon to see playback controls. You can also use the See Playback button (you won't see anything for an audio clip, despite the button's name).**

   Note that you will not see playback controls when hovering over prerecorded clips; the controls show up only with clips that you recorded using OneNote.

For advanced audio and video settings, such as to switch cameras or recording codecs, click or tap the Audio & Video Settings button to the right of the recording controls.

Extracting Text from Handwriting

Among the cooler features of OneNote are its ink technologies that enable you to use a stylus or even your finger to literally write notes on the screen. If you want to include these notes in a report or other professional document, however, you'll probably want to turn your handwriting — no matter how lovely it is — into text that can be formatted. Follow these steps to turn your ink notes into text:

1. **Open a note page with handwriting on it or use the Draw tab to write something on a blank space on a note.**

2. **Select the Draw tab if it's not selected already and click or tap the Ink to Text button.**

   OneNote automatically converts anything it sees as "text-like" into text. You can then format, copy, cut, or otherwise work with the "text" as usual. Figure 3-9 shows text before conversion (at the bottom) and after conversion (at the top). Notice that OneNote didn't pick up the "J" in my name.

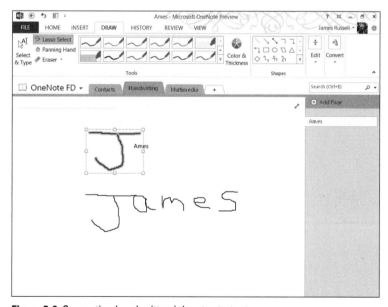

Figure 3-9: Converting handwritten ink notes to text.

Depending on your handwriting, OneNote may not recognize parts of the text and simply not convert it, just as it missed the "J" in my name in Figure 3-9. If so, follow these steps:

1. **Use the Lasso Select tool to select the text that did not convert.**

2. **Right-click or press and hold on the selected text. In the pop-up menu that appears, choose Treat Selected Ink As and then choose Handwriting from the submenu.**

3. **Next, click or tap the Ink to Text button to convert the selection to text.**

   If this doesn't work, you'll have to reenter the text manually by ink or by typing the missing text.

Creating Notes from Templates

Templates are essentially notes that are preformatted so that you can basically fill in blanks to create a professional-looking note. The following sections give you the skinny on the default OneNote templates and show you how to use them.

Discovering default OneNote templates

OneNote 2013 comes with a number of templates that you can use to quickly create new notes; these default templates fall into the following five categories:

✔ **Academic:** OneNote was designed for students to take notes, and although the program is useful for anyone, students taking notes are still a key strength of the software. These templates can show you what you can do with lecture notes, whether you want simple or advanced notes or templates specifically designed for math or history classes.

✔ **Blank:** This category includes various sizes, types, and colors of blank paper. Whether you want postcard size, legal size, or ruled paper like you see in actual notebooks, you can choose from more than a dozen sizes and styles and even change the background color of the paper.

✔ **Business:** Meeting notes are the focus of this category. Whether you want simple, personal, or formal meeting notes, these templates make it easy to take and organize your meeting notes.

✔ **Decorative:** If you want to add some pizzazz to your notes, you'll like this category, which has dozens of decorative note paper styles similar to the specialty paper you can buy in office supply stores. Most of these include graphical elements either in the title bar of the document, down the left margin, or all over the page.

✔ **Planners:** The smallest of the categories, planners include several to-do list templates that come with graphical elements and check boxes by default. Some include multiple lists separated by priority or project, as well as a single to-do list.

Creating a note using a template

Using templates in OneNote is easy and gives you a major shortcut to a nicely formatted note. Follow these steps to start a new note using a template:

1. **Open a new page in OneNote and select the Insert tab.**

2. **Click or tap the Page Templates button.**

   The Templates pane appears at the right side of the OneNote window, as shown in Figure 3-10.

Figure 3-10: The Templates pane.

If you click or tap the down arrow on the Page Templates button instead, you'll see shortcuts to templates you've used previously, as well as a shortcut at the bottom of the list to open the Templates panel. Use these shortcuts to avoid having to open the Templates pane at all.

3. **Click or tap the black downward-pointing arrow next to a category on the Templates pane to see the templates in that category.**

4. **Select the name of a template to apply it to the currently open page.**

Templates are easier to use before creating a note. To use a template on an existing note, you must create a new page using the template and then copy and paste the content from the original note over to the new page that includes the template. If you simply try to add a template to an existing note, all of the note content will be erased (although you can press Ctrl+Z to undo the action).

Creating a template

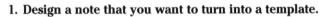

Creating a template is as simple as designing a note and saving it as a template. Follow these steps to do so:

1. **Design a note that you want to turn into a template.**

   Consider putting generic information in the template version of the note rather than specifics. For example, you can put "First Name" instead of your actual first name.

2. **Select the Insert tab and click or tap the Page Templates button.**

   The Templates pane appears at the right side of the OneNote window.

3. **With the note you want to turn into a template open, select the Save Current Page as Template link on the Templates pane.**

   A dialog box opens, prompting you to name the template. You can click the check box to make the template the default template for all new notes in the current section.

4. **Enter a name for the template and click Save.**

   If this is your first saved template, a new category called My Templates appears on the Templates pane with your new template beneath it. All future templates that you save will appear here as well.

Setting a default template

You can set a template to be the default template for all new notes in a given section. To do so, follow these steps:

1. **Open a page and apply the template that you want for that page.**

2. **Select the Insert tab and click or tap the Page Templates button.**

   The Templates pane appears at the right side of the OneNote window.

3. **Select a template from the drop-down list at the bottom of the Always Use a Specific Template section of the Templates pane.**

As soon as you close the Templates pane, OneNote forgets the default template and resorts to the No Default Template setting.

Chapter 4

Inserting External Data and Taking Quick Notes

- -

In This Chapter

▶ Taking screen captures

▶ Adding Office data to OneNote notes

▶ Working with Office data in notes

▶ Simplifying notes with quick notes

- -

*O*ne of the beautiful features of OneNote is its ability to accept file and document types of all kinds, including those from other Microsoft Office apps. Because OneNote is currently the only Office app on iOS and Android platforms, if you want to access non-OneNote Office data on those devices you can use OneNote to do so. In some cases, but not all, you can even work with that data.

In this chapter, I show you how to insert and work with file content from other major Office apps as well as how to use the Send to OneNote Tool to capture screen shots and write quick notes. Finally, I give you an overview of the essential Insert tab in OneNote 2013.

Inserting Data from Office Apps

You can insert Office documents into OneNote easily, and you have three major options available to you to do so: as a printout, as an attachment, or manually as raw data. The following sections describe how to insert data using these methods in general.

You may not be able to do much editing with the data in Office documents, if at all, especially from the mobile versions of OneNote, but you can at least access it.

Inserting data as a printout

When you insert data as a printout, OneNote treats it just like a real printout in a real binder. Because the printout is a static image, you can't edit the original document using its original formatting, but you can mark it up with ink (see Chapters 1 and 3 for more information on using ink with notes). Figure 4-1 shows a Word printout.

Although you can't edit a printout with OneNote 2013, you can search the text in the printout.

Here's how to add a Word document as a printout in your note:

1. **Open your note and place your cursor in a note page where you want the printout to appear.**

   The printout appears below and to the right of the cursor.

2. **Select the Insert tab and click or tap File Printout.**

Inserting data as file attachments

You can insert Office documents as attachments, which embeds an image of the icon for the associated Office app and the name of the file. You then double-click the icon to open it in its default app. To do so, follow these steps:

1. **Open your note and place your cursor in a note page where you want the attachment to appear.**

   The attachment appears below and to the right of the cursor.

2. **Select the Insert tab and click or tap File Attachment with the paperclip icon on it.**

   A Browse window appears.

3. **Browse to the file you want, select it, and then click or tap Insert.**

4. **Select Attach File.**

Inserting file data manually

If you want to insert individual elements of a file from another Office app into OneNote, you can. You may or may not be able to work with the item that you're pasting into OneNote, but you can get it in there; simply copy the content in the open document in the other Office app and paste it into OneNote wherever you want it.

For example, if you want to add an individual image from a Visio file, you can paste it in, but you won't be able to resize it or otherwise work with it as you can in Visio. On the other hand, if you insert text, you will be able to edit it (see the "Inserting word data as text" section later in this chapter). Figure 4-2 shows several symbols from Visio in OneNote Mobile for Android. They look cool but can't be edited other than moving or deleting them.

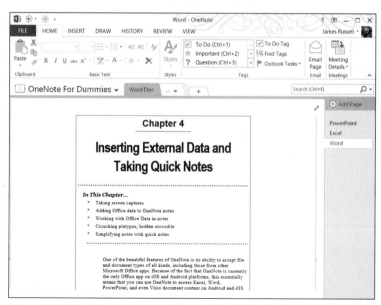

Figure 4-1: A Word document snuggling comfortably in OneNote 2013.

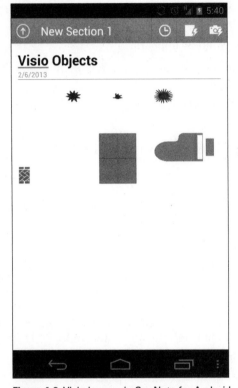

Figure 4-2: Visio images in OneNote for Android.

Managing Office Data

Manipulating the data inserted into notes from other Office apps differs depending on the app. Some apps' data, such as data from PowerPoint, can't be edited at all, whereas some data can be edited by opening the data for editing in the original app. The following sections describe how to manipulate major data types from the most popular Office apps.

Inserting word data as text

If you manually copy text from a Word document and paste it into OneNote as described earlier in the chapter, you can still edit that text in OneNote 2013 and even in other versions of OneNote, such as OneNote Mobile for iOS or Android. Following are a few tips for working with manually inserted Word data:

✔ The text retains its formatting for the most part in OneNote 2013, but as you can see in Figure 4-3, accessing it via Android strips the formatting except for some colors and highlighting.

✔ You can retain the formatting appearance even if you make changes via a more limited app such as OneNote Mobile for Android. If you keep your changes within existing lines and don't make too many new lines, the lines you do change will retain their previous format.

✔ If your document looks like dog food when you open it again in OneNote 2013, use the Format Painter to tweak formatting as necessary or, as a worst-case scenario, open the file in Word and re-edit it there.

Inserting Excel data

OneNote lets you add entire spreadsheets to notes, and you can also choose from charts or tables within the spreadsheet to add to your note individually. As long as you don't insert the data as a printout, you can even edit that data later if necessary. The following sections show you how to work with Excel data in these various ways.

Insert existing spreadsheet data

You can insert an entire sheet from Excel into your note. All cells that either have information in them or are between cells that do will be inserted. You can also choose to just add individual charts or tables from a spreadsheet. Here's how to perform these actions:

1. **Open your note and place your cursor in a note page where you want the Excel content to appear.**

   The content will appear below and to the right of the cursor.

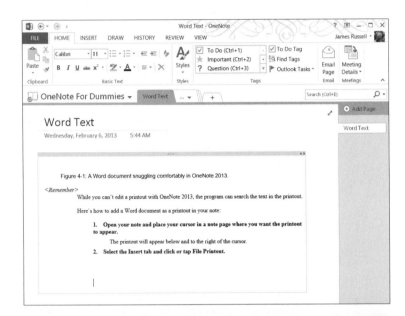

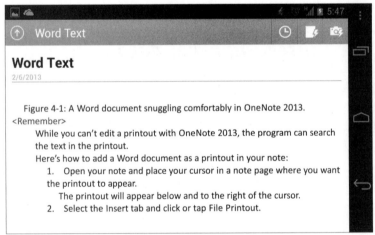

Figure 4-3: Word text in OneNote 2013 (top) and the same text in OneNote Mobile for Android (bottom).

2. **Select the Insert tab and click or tap the Excel icon and choose Existing Excel Spreadsheet from the drop-down list.**

The Excel icon won't appear in OneNote if Excel is not installed on the same PC that OneNote is installed on. If you don't have Excel on your current machine, use the File Attachment button instead.

A Browse window appears.

3. **Browse to the file you want, select it, and then click or tap Insert.**

   The Insert File window appears with several options on it.

4. **Select Insert Spreadsheet or Insert a Chart or Table.**

   If you choose Insert Spreadsheet, the spreadsheet appears in your note, and you can ignore the rest of this list.

   If you choose Insert a Chart or Table, the Custom Insert window appears, as shown in Figure 4-4, asking what you want to add. Depending on the formatting of your spreadsheet, charts or tables in the spreadsheet will have a name and number.

5. **Select the charts and/or tables that you want to appear in the note and click or tap OK.**

   The charts and/or tables you select appear in your note.

Insert new Excel content

If you're working in a note and see the need for a new spreadsheet, table, or chart, just follow these steps to create a new one right in your note:

1. **Open the note you want to add a spreadsheet, chart, or table to and position your cursor in the note where you want the content to appear.**

   The Excel content will appear below and to the right of the cursor.

Figure 4-4: The Custom Insert window helps you insert just a chart or table.

2. **On the Insert tab, click or tap the Excel icon and then choose New Excel Spreadsheet from the drop-down menu that appears.**

   A blank Excel content box appears in the note.

3. **Open Excel by clicking or tapping Edit, which is located at the upper left of the drawing.**

4. **Create your spreadsheet, chart, or table and then click or tap Save in Excel to save it and close Excel.**

   The new Excel content appears in the formerly empty box in OneNote.

Editing Excel data

As long as you don't insert Excel data as a printout, you can edit it after it has been inserted into or created in your note. To edit Excel data, follow these steps:

1. **Right-click or press and hold on the spreadsheet, chart, or table in your note and choose Edit from the menu that appears.**

   Excel opens the content for editing.

2. **Edit the spreadsheet, chart, or table in Excel and click or tap Save in Excel to save it and close Excel.**

   The spreadsheet updates itself in OneNote.

Inserting data from Outlook

You can insert Outlook e-mail data into a OneNote page, but you have to do so from Outlook rather than from OneNote. Here's how to insert an e-mail from Outlook:

1. **Open Outlook and select the e-mail you want to add to your note.**

2. **Click or tap the OneNote button in the Move section of the Outlook Home tab.**

   Instead of Steps 1 and 2 above, you can also right-click or press and hold on an e-mail and choose OneNote from the context menu that appears.

   The Select Location in OneNote window appears asking which notebook, section, and page you want to add the e-mail to.

3. **Browse to the note you want to insert the e-mail into and then click or tap OK.**

   The e-mail is pasted into your note with formatting intact and header information inserted into a small table at the top.

Inserting Visio diagrams

You can insert Visio diagrams into a note and retain the ability to edit it as long as you don't insert the diagram as a printout, which effectively creates a static image of the diagram. The following sections give you the basics of adding diagrams to OneNote and then editing them.

Inserting an existing diagram

Here's how to insert a Visio document as an image:

1. **Open your note and place your cursor in a note page where you want the diagram to appear.**

   The diagram appears below and to the right of the cursor.

2. **Select the Insert tab, click or tap the Visio icon, and choose Existing Visio Drawing from the drop-down menu.**

   The Visio icon only appears in OneNote if Visio is installed on the same PC that OneNote is installed on. If you don't have Visio on your current machine, the icon won't appear; use the File Attachment button instead if this is the case.

   A Browse window appears.

3. **Browse to and select your file and then click or tap Insert.**

   The Insert File window appears, as shown in Figure 4-5.

4. **Select Insert Diagram and click or tap Insert.**

Figure 4-5: Inserting a Visio diagram.

Creating a diagram in OneNote

If you're working in a note and see the need for a Visio diagram, just follow these steps to create a new diagram right in your note:

1. **Open the note you want to add a diagram to and position your cursor in the note where you want the diagram to appear.**

   The diagram will appear below and to the right of the cursor.

2. **On the Insert tab, click or tap the Visio icon and then choose New Visio Drawing from the drop-down menu.**

   A blank Visio drawing appears in the note.

3. **Click or tap Edit at the upper left of the drawing to open Visio.**

4. **Create your diagram and then click or tap Save in Visio to save the diagram and close Visio.**

   The new drawing appears in the formerly empty diagram box in OneNote.

Editing Visio diagrams

As long as you don't insert a Visio diagram as a printout, you can edit it after it's created in or inserted into your note. To edit a diagram, follow these steps:

1. **Right-click or press and hold on the diagram in your note and choose Edit from the menu that appears.**

   Visio opens the diagram for editing.

2. **Edit the diagram in Visio and click or tap Save to save it and close Visio.**

   The diagram updates itself in OneNote.

Adding External Data with the Send to OneNote Tool

Over the course of OneNote releases, the Send to OneNote Tool grew from being a simple tool for clipping, or saving, a portion of a screen to include in a note or to share with others to being a tool that you can use for sending information from one program to another or for starting a quick note.

Checking out the OneNote tool interface

The Send to OneNote Tool interface includes three buttons and a couple of links. By default, the tool starts when you start OneNote, has its own system tray icon, and even has its own taskbar icon for easy access. Figure 4-6 shows all of these features.

Figure 4-6: The Send to OneNote Tool and its taskbar and system tray icons.

 If you've turned it off, you can open the Send to OneNote Tool by selecting the View tab and clicking or tapping the Send to OneNote Tool button. On a keyboard, you can also press Windows+N.

As you can see from the figure, there are three big buttons on the tool, plus an Exit link and a check box that you can check or uncheck depending on whether you want the tool to start when you start OneNote. The buttons are as follows:

- ✔ **Screen Clipping:** Use this tool to open the clipping tool, which allows you to capture all or part of the PC screen to add to OneNote or share with others. See the next section for information on capturing screen clippings and sharing them.

- ✔ **Send to OneNote:** The icon for this tool changes significantly depending on where you are. Figure 4-7 shows how the tool looks when viewing from Internet Explorer Excel, PowerPoint, and Word, respectively. You'll see the last icon if you can't send anything currently open on your desktop. For example, if you only have Microsoft Paint open, you'll see this grayed-out icon. If you also have Word open in addition to Paint, you'll see the Word icon, even if Word isn't the app you're currently viewing.

- ✔ **New Quick Note:** Quick notes allow you to jot down a note that you don't want to worry about organizing yet. See the "Taking quick notes" section near the end of the chapter for information about quick notes and how to use them effectively.

Figure 4-7: The various faces of the Send to OneNote button.

With the Send to OneNote Tool open, press S to open the clipping tool, D to send the currently open Office content to OneNote, or N to start a new quick note.

Capturing screen clippings

Screen captures, or clippings, are useful in all sorts of cases, from showing someone your favorite desktop background to creating documentation — even books such as this one — that shows things that may be hard for your readers to visualize and to help them orient themselves to the tasks you're discussing.

Although for years you've been able to capture a screenshot with the Print Screen keyboard button, you can capture only the entire screen with that key or press Alt+Print Screen to capture just the active window. Those were your two choices.

With the Screen Clipping tool in OneNote, you can highlight just the part of the screen you want to capture and grab it so that you don't have an extra step of cropping out parts of the screen or window that you don't want. You are thus essentially cropping the shot as you take it. Here's how:

1. **Summon the Send to OneNote Tool and click or tap the Screen Clipping button (or just press S with the tool open).**

   The entire screen grays out, and crosshairs appear.

2. **Use your mouse or finger to move the crosshairs to the very upper left of the portion of the screen you want to capture.**

   Everything in the box you create as you drag down and right around will be in full color instead of grayed out like the rest of the screen, as shown in Figure 4-8; the image will be composed of the area you capture.

Figure 4-8: Capturing a screen.

3. **Click or tap and then drag the crosshairs down and to the right until the whole image you want to capture appears; then release the mouse button or lift your finger from the screen.**

   The Select Location in OneNote window appears above your image, as shown in Figure 4-9.

4. **Choose one of the following to complete your screen capture:**

   • **Send to Selected Location:** Select a note within the large field near the top of the window and then click or tap this button to send the screen capture there.

   • **Copy to Clipboard:** To paste the image manually into a note or to another location, click or tap this button, which copies the image to the Clipboard for use in Paint or other graphics programs.

   Near the bottom of the window is a check box that says "Don't Ask Me Again and Always Do the Following." If you're finding that you're always adding screen clippings to the same location, select this box to avoid having to choose the location each time. You can always go to the Send to OneNote section in OneNote's options and reverse this choice.

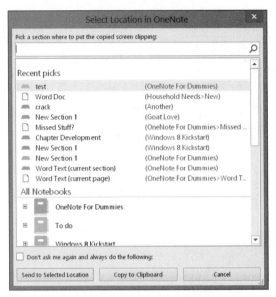

Figure 4-9: The Select Location in OneNote window.

Inserting data via the Send to OneNote Tool

When you use the Send to OneNote Tool to insert data into a note, the tool assumes you want a printout of the file, not an attached file. If there are only two choices for that data, there aren't any extra steps involved — the data is inserted immediately as a printout. If you try to insert data from an app that has more than the two choices for inserting, a pop-up window appears asking which type of format you want to use to insert the data. For example, in Excel, OneNote asks the question because Excel has a third option for inserting a chart.

You can send also send web pages to OneNote in this way. To do so, open the web page in your browser, open the Send to OneNote Tool, and press the Send to OneNote button.

Taking quick notes

Quick notes allow you to jot something down quickly without haggling with the organizational structure of OneNote. Later, you can go back to the unfiled quick note and figure out where to put it. The following sections describe the basics of working with quick notes.

Accessing quick notes

You can access quick notes from the Send to OneNote Tool or by choosing Quick Notes from the notebook drop-down list in OneNote 2013. If you do the latter, you won't see the Pages tab described in the next section; instead the note will open in the regular OneNote 2013 interface.

Checking out the Quick Notes Pages tab

When writing a quick note for the first time, the quick note has its own slightly unique interface. By default you won't see a ribbon at all, but if you click or tap the three dots at the top of the window you'll see the Ribbon and that it includes a Pages tab on the Ribbon; Figure 4-10 shows the Pages tab.

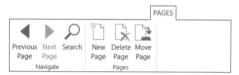

Figure 4-10: The Pages tab on the Quick Notes Ribbon.

Following are the items you see on the tab; the first three are in the Navigate section, and the latter three are in the Pages section:

- ✔ **Previous Page:** From the one that's currently displayed, go to the previous quick note.

- ✔ **Next Page:** From the one that you're currently viewing, go to the next quick note.

- ✔ **Search:** Search notes — not just quick notes.

- ✔ **New Page:** Create a new quick note page.

- ✔ **Delete Page:** Delete the currently open quick note page.

- ✔ **Move Page:** Move the currently open quick note page.

Creating a quick note

You have two options for creating a new quick note:

- ✔ Open the Send to OneNote Tool and click or tap the New Quick Note button (or press N).

- ✔ Choose New Page while viewing the Pages tab with a quick note currently open after having started a previous new quick note.

Whichever option you choose, a new note opens, as shown in Figure 4-11.

Figure 4-11: A simplified note interface for quick notes.

By default, quick notes have a simple interface with the following items not typical of regular note:

✔ A lavender background

✔ No title or date

✔ A row of buttons on the top row that you can click or tap to access the Ribbon

✔ A double-arrow icon in the upper right that you can choose to view the note in the full OneNote 2013 interface

You can take notes just as you do with any other note. Essentially, you're looking at the same options, just with a simplified interface and organized under the Quick Notes section of your Personal (web) folder rather than within the greater OneNote structure.

Filing quick notes

You can file quick notes with the Move Page item on the Pages Ribbon or any other way you move or copy notes (refer to Chapter 2).

Inserting External Data with the Insert Tab

Although I discuss the various items on the Insert tab at the appropriate time in other chapters, it's a good idea to at least become familiar with what's on it now (see Figure 4-12).

Figure 4-12: The OneNote 2013 Insert tab.

The following list identifies the sections on the Insert tab and the commands on those sections:

- ✔ **Insert:** The section has a single item on it: Insert Space. Use this option to increase space between elements that you think are crammed together or that need other items between them.

- ✔ **Tables:** This section also sports a single item: Table. Click or tap this item to insert a table.

- ✔ **Files:** Use to insert various types of files, from attachments to printouts, spreadsheets, and diagrams.

- ✔ **Images:** Use to insert screen captures, pictures, online images, and scanned art.

- ✔ **Links:** Use to insert a link to an online source.

- ✔ **Recording:** Use to insert video and audio as searchable parts of your notes (refer to Chapter 3).

- ✔ **Time Stamp:** Use to insert date, time, or date and time stamps.

- ✔ **Pages:** Use to insert a page template to help you format your notes.

- ✔ **Symbols:** Use to insert mathematical equations or other symbols.

Chapter 5

Securing and Managing Notes with SkyDrive

*S*kyDrive is a cloud storage service that you can access from any web-enabled device. The key to saving and accessing your notes from anywhere is to sync those notes in the cloud via SkyDrive. Additionally, you just can't perform some basic functions on mobile versions of OneNote that you can using SkyDrive.

How you manage notes via SkyDrive differs depending on which device and method you use to access the service. Because SkyDrive is accessible via web browsers and apps for Windows 8 and Windows 7/Vista/XP, OS X, Android, iOS, and Windows Phone devices, you have at least two options for accessing SkyDrive, depending on the device or PC you're using.

Related to note management is note security, so in this chapter I show you how to obtain and use SkyDrive on whatever device you're using as well as how to password-protect notes using OneNote 2013.

Getting SkyDrive on Your Device

Smartphones and tablet devices are becoming as prevalent in today's computing environment as PCs and, in some cases, are replicating PC functionality. In the case of SkyDrive, the SkyDrive web interface is by far the most feature-rich version of the service, but you can perform many of the same functions — not all, but many — using your tablet or smartphone via its dedicated SkyDrive app.

If you can't beat 'em, join 'em

Microsoft's CEO, Steve Ballmer, has made many public statements about how much he loathes the Android operating system, and indeed the company for years refused to support the platform at all. Microsoft was similarly slow to create apps for Apple's iOS operating system that runs iPhone and iPad — both iOS and Android are major competitors to Microsoft's own Windows Phone operating system. Ninety percent of the world uses the Windows operating system, but the same is not the case for the Windows Phone operating system — as of this writing, Windows Phone has less than 3-percent market share. In short, people use whichever smartphone they want to use, and most of them don't use Windows Phone devices.

Microsoft is a software company, in the end, and as the iOS and Android platforms began taking off and gaining millions of users, the potential to monetize iOS and Android users became undeniable. This is especially true given that Microsoft owns patents related to Android which generates royalties. Further, OneNote's main competitor, EverNote, is on iOS and Android, and so by continuing to deny iPhone, iPad, and Android users access to OneNote, Microsoft was, in effect, crippling the potential of the app.

Starting in late 2011, Microsoft quietly bit the bullet and started releasing a slew of apps for Android — Ballmer's screaming aside. Now that OneNote is on iOS and Android — and users who don't have OneNote at all can read and edit notes via a free web-based interface — Microsoft is ensuring consumers can access their notes on all three major mobile platforms.

Microsoft has created SkyDrive apps for various device platforms to make working with the service even easier. You can visit `https://apps.live.com/skydrive` for links to at least some of the following apps; the listings below include direct links, as well.

- ✔ **Windows 8/RT:** Microsoft has released a special, touch-centric version of SkyDrive as a Windows Store app that is installed on Windows 8 and Windows RT by default.

  Windows Store apps is Microsoft's term for apps designed to run from only the Windows 8 Start screen, not as desktop applications that run on Windows 7 or earlier versions of Windows.

- ✔ **Windows Desktop Utility:** Windows 8 and older versions of Windows have a SkyDrive app that adds the SkyDrive folder to Windows Explorer or File Explorer, as I discuss later in the "Managing notebooks with File Explorer or Windows Explorer" later in this chapter. You can get the SkyDrive app

for Windows 8, Windows 7, and Windows Vista at `http://
windows.microsoft.com/en-US/skydrive/download`.

✔ **Windows Phone 7 and 8:** Versions 7.5 and 8 of the Windows
Phone have a dedicated SkyDrive app; you can obtain it at the
Windows Store.

✔ **Mac:** The SkyDrive app for OS X creates a folder in your Finder
that you can sync folders to. You can then work with files and
folders just as with any other folder on your Mac. You can get
the Mac SkyDrive app at `https://apps.live.com/sky
drive/app/f644a8ef-9f98-4d1b-a3d2-eab969b0fd44`.

✔ **iOS:** This app runs on iPad, iPhone, and iPod touch devices.
Search for *SkyDrive* in the App Store and install the service
from there.

✔ **Android:** The SkyDrive Android runs on Android smartphones and tablets running version 2.3 or later of the operating system. Search for *SkyDrive* in the Google Play store and
install the service as you would any other app.

The following sections show you how to access SkyDrive on your
device; later in the "Managing Notebooks on SkyDrive" section I
show you how to manage notes and other files on various devices.

Managing Notebooks on SkyDrive

Unlocking the power of OneNote mobile apps involves using
SkyDrive. In particular, you must use SkyDrive to manage your
notes when OneNote doesn't have the required features available, as is the case with the Android version of OneNote Mobile.
Familiarizing yourself with the various interfaces of SkyDrive, then,
helps you make the most of OneNote.

The following sections describe how to manage your notes via
SkyDrive on the major platforms that the service is on.

Managing notebooks with the Windows 8 SkyDrive app

The Windows 8–style SkyDrive app is installed by default as a tile
on the Start screen. The first time you access the tile, you may
have to log in with your Microsoft account. After you do so, the
SkyDrive app appears, as shown in Figure 5-1.

Figure 5-1: The Windows 8–style SkyDrive app.

As you can see from the figure, folders appear as images with blue boxes at the bottom of each with a number showing how many files are in the folder. Files that aren't in folders are to the right of the folders (not visible in the figure).

Here's how to manage files and folders with the app:

1. **Click or tap a folder tile to open it and view its contents.**

2. **Click or tap a file to open it in its default app or viewer.**

3. **Select the Back button at the upper left of the screen to go back a screen, which equates to going up one folder.**

   If you don't see a Back button, you're in the top SkyDrive folder.

4. **Select the down-pointing arrow next to the heading *YourName*'s SkyDrive at the top of the screen in your root folder to drop down a menu via which you can access files in Recent Documents or Shared folders.**

5. **Right-click or press and hold on a file or folder to summon a bar at the bottom of the screen with options on it.**

   The following list shows the possible options; the first four will be visible at the left side of the bar if a file is selected;

you'll only see Clear Selection and Manage if a folder is selected.

- **Clear Selection:** Deselect the current item or items that are selected.

Unlike when working with files in File Explorer or Windows Explorer, if you select one or more files and then click or tap it a second time — even after a few seconds — you'll open the file with the default program instead of deselecting it. The Clear Selection button gives you a way to get around this.

- **Download:** Use this item to download a file on SkyDrive to your local device.

- **Manage:** Here you'll find the important Rename, Delete, and Move options.

- **Open With:** Select this button to view or change the app with which the current file opens.

- **Refresh:** If you've made changes that aren't appearing, use this button to refresh the current view.

- **New Folder:** Create a new folder in the current location.

- **Upload:** Select this option to choose a file from your computer to upload to SkyDrive.

- **Details/Thumbnails:** Toggle between seeing simple thumbnails and seeing details about each file.

- **Select All:** Select all items in the current view.

Managing notebooks with File Explorer or Windows Explorer

The program named Windows Explorer in Windows 95 through Windows 7 was renamed *File Explorer* in Windows 8. File Explorer has a slew of new interface additions and options for working with your files, but SkyDrive is available in both after you install the Windows Desktop SkyDrive app and functions the same in File Explorer and Windows Explorer.

After installing the utility, a SkyDrive item appears under the Favorites heading in the left pane of File Explorer or Windows Explorer, as shown in Figure 5-2.

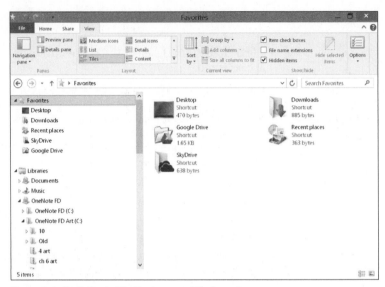

Figure 5-2: SkyDrive in File Explorer on Windows 8.

Following are some tips for working with SkyDrive via File Explorer or Windows Explorer:

- The contents of your SkyDrive appear in folders or files. Work with them as you work with other folders or files on your hard drive. They sync almost immediately when you change them as long as you're connected to the Internet. If you're not, they sync when you connect.

- Click in the Search SkyDrive field at the upper right and enter a search term to search for files or folders.

- Right-click or press and hold on the SkyDrive folder or any folder within it, choose Include in Library, and then select a library to share that folder in one of your Explorer libraries.

Managing notebooks with SkyDrive on the web

Because SkyDrive is cloud-accessible, even if you don't have a SkyDrive app installed on the device, you can access the service from whatever device you're using as long as it supports a functional web browser.

SkyDrive on the web is the single most-functional interface the service has available on any platform. Use SkyDrive on the web on computers that don't have SkyDrive available or if you want to get more storage or configure advanced options.

Here's how to access SkyDrive using a web browser:

1. **Fire up your favorite web browser and navigate to** www.skydrive.com.

   The SkyDrive log in page appears.

2. **Input your username and password and select Sign In.**

   Your SkyDrive interface appears, as shown in Figure 5-3.

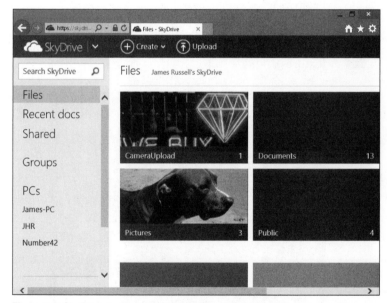

Figure 5-3: SkyDrive for the web has more features than any other version.

Following are some notes on using SkyDrive for the web that differentiate it from the other interfaces:

- ✔ **Chat:** Here you can access Windows Live chats and Facebook chats if you have Facebook tied to your Microsoft account.

- ✔ **Options:** Here you can access the following options that you can't access in any other interface for SkyDrive:

  - **Manage Storage/Upgrade:** Here you can get more storage if the free 7GB you get aren't enough.

- **Office File Formats:** Decide between Microsoft and Open Document formats for new Excel, Word, and PowerPoint docs.

- **People Tagging:** Decide who can tag you or others in your photos.

Managing notebooks with SkyDrive for iOS

SkyDrive for iOS devices allows you to access your files from your iPhone, iPad, or iPod touch devices. After signing in, SkyDrive appears with the Settings menu open, as shown on the iPad in Figure 5-4.

The interface will look decidedly smushed on an iPhone or iPod touch in comparison to on an iPad, but the app includes the same features.

Figure 5-4: SkyDrive on iPad 2 with the Settings menu open.

Note the following when working with SkyDrive on your iOS device:

✔ **View buttons:** Across the middle of the bottom bar of the app, you see four buttons; you can use the first three buttons to change your file view. The three buttons in the middle of this lower bar allow you to see your files. From left to right, these buttons are Files, Recent, and Shared.

✔ **Settings:** The gear wheel button at the very right of the bottom bar is the ill-named Settings button; there is only one item on this list that you can change. Here you see which account you're in, your available storage, and links to the app's privacy statement, terms, and help resources. The only item you can change is under Photo Uploads, where you choose whether your photos are uploaded resized to save space or full size.

✔ **Edit/add button:** The button at the upper right of the SkyDrive interface lets you edit or add files. Choosing to add a file allows you to create folders, take new photos to add using the built-in camera, and choose existing photos to upload from your device.

Most of the file-editing features are actually available when you tap a file (see the following bullet) — using this option only allows you to move or delete files, but this is the only place where you can do so with multiple files. Use the radio buttons to select files and then tap the Move or Delete button to perform that action.

✔ **File options:** Tapping a file opens it in its own screen. Tap the screen, and you'll see buttons appear at the top and bottom of the screen: The left-facing arrow at the upper left takes you back to the main SkyDrive interface, whereas the four buttons at the bottom of the screen let you work with the file.

From left to right, the buttons on the bottom of the screen let you share a file, change its permissions, copy a hyperlink for it to the Clipboard (choose from a link that allows viewing only or viewing and editing), delete the file, move the file, or either rename the file or open it in another app.

The onscreen buttons disappear after a moment — just touch the screen again to bring them back.

Managing notebooks with SkyDrive for Android

SkyDrive on Android is fairly basic, but you can perform most basic management services for your notes using the app. After you set up the app from the Google Play store, you must log in with your Microsoft account. The SkyDrive app interface appears. Figure 5-5 shows the app on a Nexus 4 phone.

Just as with the iOS version of SkyDrive, the Android app appears larger on a tablet, but the functions are the same.

Keep the following in mind when working with the SkyDrive Android app:

- ✔ **View buttons:** In the blue bar at the top is a drop-down list that allows you to switch views between your main files, recent documents, and documents shared with you.

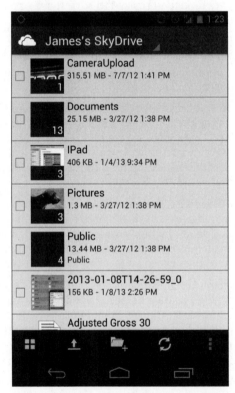

Figure 5-5: SkyDrive on a Nexus 4 Android phone.

✓ **Function buttons:** The icons across the bottom allow you to perform various functions such as switching between list and thumbnails views, uploading new files, creating a folder, refreshing your view, and viewing your settings. Settings let you see which account you're in, your available storage, and links to the app's privacy statement, terms, and help resources. You can change the upload or download settings depending on whether you want your photos full size when uploaded or downloaded or resized to save data usage and space.

✓ **File management:** Tap a file, and it will open in full-screen mode with a link at the top showing the filename that doubles as a Back button and five icons across the bottom that allow you to delete, copy a link to, download, share, or rename a file. Downloaded files will be stored in the SkyDrive folder on your phone's SD card if your phone has one or on an internal SD card if it doesn't have one, as is the case with the Nexus 4. You can choose the link you copy so that the recipient can only view the file or can edit as well as view it.

Managing notebooks with SkyDrive for other platforms

Microsoft has made SkyDrive available on more devices than are possible to cover in this book — one that's supposed to be about OneNote, no less — but I do want to note SkyDrive features on two of those platforms that may eventually appear on the major platforms:

✓ **Windows Phone:** Versions 7 and 8 of the platform have SkyDrive functionality and apps, and version 3.0 of the SkyDrive app for the OS (see the magnifying glass in Figure 5-6) has a search function that you can use to search your SkyDrive for files or folders. As of this writing, a search function is not available in the iOS or Android apps.

✓ **Xbox 360:** This version of SkyDrive is focused on photos and movies, namely because the console cannot handle other file types, but there are a couple cool features worth mention:

  • *(Nearly) Instant view photos:* Using your Windows Phone, you can snap photos and have them almost instantly appear on your TV by syncing a folder on your phone to your SkyDrive.

  • *Kinect controls:* The Xbox version of SkyDrive also supports Kinect voice controls and gestures, making it the only version of the app that you can use via voice or motion gestures.

Figure 5-6: Viewing SkyDrive on a Windows Phone.

Part II
Taking Notes via Other OneNote Versions

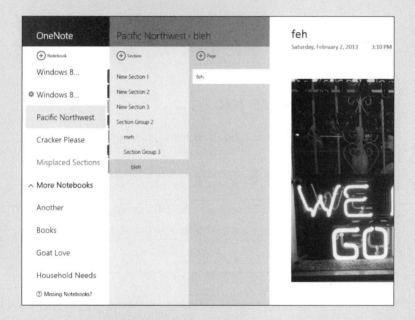

Learn how to use OneNote 2013 on various devices by going to www.dummies.com/extras/onenote2013.

In this part . . .

✔ Find out how to access and edit notes no matter what devices you use.

✔ Get familiar with the touch revolution with OneNote for Windows 8.

✔ Learn how to edit notes on Android and iOS devices.

✔ Discover how you can manage notes with OneNote Web App.

Chapter 6

Taking Notes with OneNote for Windows 8

*O*neNote for Windows 8 was created from the ground up using the Windows Store environment, previously called Metro, which refers essentially to the Start screen and the tiled apps that work only on Windows 8 or Windows RT. These apps are written using Web technologies, take up the entire screen, and typically scroll left to right instead of up and down. OneNote for Windows 8 is the first Office app to be created in this new style.

OneNote for Windows 8 can be very useful and has some features not found in OneNote 2013; however, it's really more like a preview of the next version of Office — and OneNote — than a go-to version of OneNote, which is OneNote 2013. Namely, OneNote for Windows 8 is incomplete in many ways compared to its cousin OneNote 2013 (see the nearby sidebar), and OneNote for Windows 8 defers to OneNote 2013 for many functions. Still, the app is functional for note-taking, especially with a touchscreen PC and devices such as Surface Pro that have ink capabilities.

In this chapter, I show you how to use OneNote for Windows 8 to take notes. I particularly focus on the concept of radial menus, which replace the tried-and-true context menus so prevalent on the Windows desktop, and I show you how to use the touchscreen-based app interface.

How the Windows Store version differs from OneNote 2013

OneNote for Windows 8, the unofficial name for the version of OneNote that runs only on Windows 8 and Windows RT, includes one feature that OneNote 2013 doesn't: radial menus (these are discussed a bit later in this chapter). Other than that, the app is missing a lot of features, such as the ability to share from the app. Additionally, although OneNote for Windows 8 is the only other version of OneNote to support ink as of this writing, its ink support is less than it is in OneNote 2013: you have four favorite pens to choose from, three thicknesses, and fewer colors. Speaking of highlighters, as of this writing there are *none* available in OneNote for Windows 8, although you can highlight text as described in the "Modifying and manipulating text" section later in this chapter.

I can go on, but I think you get the idea — OneNote for Windows 8 is an unfinished recreation of OneNote that can be useful but just isn't up to the standard of OneNote 2013 by a long shot — yet.

Navigating the OneNote for Windows 8 Interface

The experience of navigating the OneNote for Windows 8 interface is different from navigating the interface of any other Office app. The following sections get you up to speed on how to efficiently use the new touch-based interface.

Scrolling from left to right

OneNote for Windows 8, as a Windows Store–style app, shuns the *scroll up and down* paradigm that permeates Windows 7 apps and embraces instead the *scroll left to right* concept that Windows Store apps use. So, when you start OneNote for Windows 8, you see your list of notebooks at the left, a list of sections to the right, and a list of note pages to the right of that list. Farther to the right is the currently open note page. Figure 6-1 shows the default OneNote for Windows 8 interface with my notes.

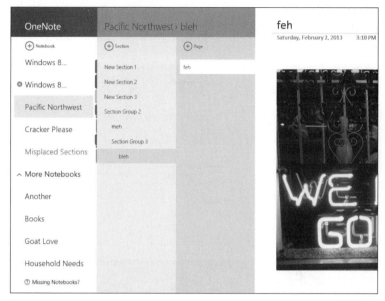

Figure 6-1: OneNote for Windows 8.

Checking out key navigation tools

As in all Windows Store apps, the key navigation items are almost always found on the options bar at the bottom of the screen (or in some cases at the top) that you access by swiping your finger down from the top of the screen, swiping up from the bottom of the screen, or by right-clicking anywhere on the screen.

The following list describes how to navigate OneNote for Windows 8 using the options bar, which in this app appears only at the bottom of the screen, as shown in Figure 6-2.

✔ **Moving back and forward:** When you access the options bar, you'll sometimes see Back and Forward buttons, which you can tap or click to go back to the note you were looking at or forward to the note you just moved back from. The moves you can make, of course, depend on how many places you've moved backward or forward. The buttons are grayed out when you first start the app.

You can tap or click Back again and again until you get back to your original place; the same applies to going forward.

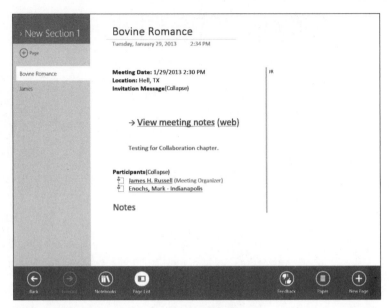

Figure 6-2: The options bar in OneNote for Windows 8.

✔ **The Navigate button on the options bar:** If a lot of items are on the options bar, the Back and Forward buttons disappear and become the Navigate button. Right-click or press and hold on a page or section name to see the button. Other buttons that may appear are described in the last section of the chapter.

✔ **Hiding or showing the page list:** Tap or click the Page List button on the options bar to show or hide the page list at the left side of the screen — the Pages column moves to the left after you open a note and the Notebooks and Sections columns are hidden.

✔ **Getting back to the list of notebooks:** If the page list is at the left side of the note page screen, simply tap or click the page name at the top to go back to viewing the columns of lists of notebooks, sections, and pages. If the page list isn't visible, you can instead access the options bar at the bottom of the screen and then tap or click the Notebooks button. Tap or click the Notebooks button again to hide the columns.

If you can't get the keyboard to stop harassing you on Surface Pro or a similar device, tap the keyboard button on the on-screen keyboard and choose the rightmost keyboard item (it's totally blank and has a down-pointing arrow) to get the keyboard to finally *go away*.

Context menus suck

In context menus, which are used in the desktop mode in Windows 8 and solely in all versions of Windows before Windows 8, submenus *fly out* to one side as you hover the mouse over them. With multiple submenus, the result is pretty bulky and hogs a lot of screen space, as shown in the following figure.

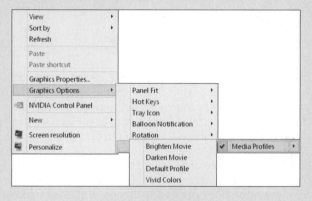

Introducing Radial Menus

Radial menus are not new in computing; they actually date back to 1969. However, they're new to Microsoft Office with their appearance in OneNote for Windows 8. The following sections describe what a radial menu is, why radial menus are a good replacement for regular context menus, and how to use them.

Comprehending radial menus

Radial menus are circular windows with multiple options around the perimeter of the circle; tap or click one and, if the item is itself a choice, an action occurs; if, on the other hand, the item leads to more choices, the circle is replaced with a submenu. In the middle of the circle is a button that either takes you back to the previous radial menu or closes the menu. The result is a menu that never takes up any more space than a single circle.

The radial menu most commonly seen in OneNote for Windows 8 is the Page menu. As you can see from Figure 6-3, dark-purple edges with a white arrow pointing outward from the circle indicate links to another radial menu, whereas plain light-pink edges indicate terminal choices or no choice at all.

Figure 6-3: The OneNote Page radial menu.

Some items, such as Bold text, are toggled on and off. If an item is toggled on, a thin purple line is visible just inside the outer circle between the outer circle and the item icon. If you hover your mouse over the icon or swipe your finger over it, the line gets a little darker. If an item is toggled off, you won't see the purple line.

Here's an example of how radial menus work: If you click or tap the Camera item at the top of the Page menu, camera-related choices appear in a new radial menu, but if you instead select the Table item on the main Page menu, a new table is inserted in the document and the Page menu closes. The Camera item leads to a submenu, as indicated by the purple border and the white arrow; the Table item is a terminal choice, as indicated by its light-pink border without an arrow.

Tapping or clicking a terminal option sometimes causes the current menu to close and a button indicating another, more relevant menu to appear, which is the case with the Table item on the Page menu. Click the Table item on the Page menu, and that menu closes. Where the Page menu was, you now see a Table menu button, which indicates that you can click or tap it to open the Table radial menu and access table-related options. You can read more about tables in the "Adding Tags and Items" section later in this chapter.

Navigating radial menus

Now that you know what radial menus are, it's time to learn how to use them. Navigating radial menus is simple and intuitive once you get used to it.

You have several choices for navigating the OneNote for Windows 8 radial menus, as described in the list below and shown in Figure 6-4:

✔ **Tapping or clicking:** Perhaps the most obvious way to work with radial menus is to tap or click items on them or to do so on the little white arrows at the edges.

✔ **Swiping through:** To open a submenu, swipe your finger from the center of the menu through the white arrow for the desired submenu.

✔ **Circling:** Using your finger, circle a menu item, and a little text box appears next to your finger showing the option you've circled; the text box indicates the option you will choose when you lift your finger.

Practice circling around multiple options to see how you can cancel one choice and choose another before lifting your finger. If you were to follow the finger-drawing path shown in Figure 6-4, for example, you'd end up with the Phone Call item.

Certain menu items, such as List and Tag, change their icons to your choice when you choose an item from the submenu. For example, the default item for the Tag submenu is the To Do tag, but if you choose the Important tag from the menu, the next time you access the menu, you'll see a star instead of the To Do box as the menu option's icon.

I discuss specific radial menus in the next section.

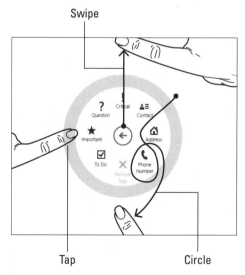

Figure 6-4: Tap, swipe, or circle an option with your finger to select it.

Identifying various radial menus

Microsoft lists nine types of radial menus in its rather sparse and dated documentation for OneNote for Windows 8, but I've been able to find only the following eight in the newest version and the ninth, labeled Insert, may just have been folded into the Page menu. Whatever the case, these are the radial menus I've been able to find:

✔ **Page:** On this menu, you find options to add tags, lists, tables, or photos, making it the most essential menu for adding items. Tap or click any blank spot on a page to summon this menu.

✔ **Note Container:** This menu gives you options to format the contents of a note container. The menu includes text color and other font options as well as highlighter options. This menu appears when you select the header bar of a container.

A *note container* surrounds every item on your note *except* ink, which can overlay or sit behind any note container. When you click or tap an item, the surrounding note container appears with a header bar that you can click or press and hold on to drag the item anywhere on the note page that you want.

✔ **Text:** Here you'll find options for text as described in the "Modifying and manipulating text" section later in this chapter. Select some text to highlight it, and this menu will appear.

✔ **Picture:** This menu has just a few options, with the only real picture-related item being Rotate, which rotates an image 90 degrees to the right. Select an image to summon this menu.

✔ **Embedded File:** This menu is noteworthy because it has Open and Open With commands so that you can either open the file in its default program or choose another program to open it with. Other than those options, though, this menu has the same basic options as the Ink menu. Select an embedded file to bring up this menu.

✔ **Table:** This menu appears when you have multiple cells highlighted and includes essentially the same options as the Text menu.

✔ **Table Insertion:** This menu appears when your cursor is in one cell with nothing highlighted. Table-specific options live here, including adding or deleting rows or columns and table sorting.

✔ **Ink:** This menu includes items for four pens, each of which can be of three thicknesses and multiple colors. Also here is an Undo item that allows you to undo the last item you wrote or redo the last item you undid.

Selecting Items

As mentioned in the previous section, to get the relevant radial menus to appear, you need to select the item you want to work with. Depending on your user interface — mouse, finger, or pen — selecting items is a different process. The following sections describe how to select items with each of these interfaces.

In all cases, when you select more than one item at the same time, you may not get the relevant radial menu that you want. For example, if you select a table, a photo, and an ink item, you will probably get the Note Container menu whether you want it or not. It takes some skill to select only what you want, especially if you have many different items crammed together and are working with your finger.

Selecting with a mouse

Selecting items with a mouse is the same as selecting any item in the Windows desktop environment with a mouse: Simply hold down the left-mouse button and lasso the item you want to work with. There are variations on this. For example, to select more than one table cell, you click in a table cell, hold down the left mouse button, and drag to the right or left or up and down to highlight more than one cell. To select text, you simply click next to the text, hold down the left-mouse button, and move to the left or right until the text you want is selected. After you've selected, or highlighted, whatever you want to work with, a relevant radial menu appears, and you can work with it using your mouse. You can also right-click the highlighted text, cells, photo, or other item to access the options bar at the bottom of the page. This tried-and-true mouse interface applies in full to OneNote for Windows 8.

Selecting with the pen button

If you hold the pen like . . . well, like a pen, you'll find the pen button under your forefinger, and you press the button with your forefinger. You select items to move, delete, or otherwise transform as follows:

1. **Grasp the pen normally, press the pen button, and encircle an item on the note page.**

   A thin outline appears around everything you select, and a button appears, depending on what you selected. For some items, including images and ink, a circle with a four-way-arrow symbol appears on the actual item as well, as long as your device is touch-enabled.

2. **Touch the menu button with the pen's tip to open a radial menu or touch the four-way-arrow symbol to move an item.**

   The item moves, and the radial menu button moves with it, which you can use after moving the item.

3. **Hover the tip of the pen over your device's screen to access the Ink radial menu and touch items on the menu with the tip of the pen to access submenus.**

   The Ink radial menu includes items for your four favorite pens as well as Undo and Redo as described in the "Identifying various radial menus" section earlier in this chapter.

Selecting with your finger

Selecting items with your finger is more like selecting with the pen button, described in the previous section, than it is to selecting with a mouse. When you tap within a note somewhere other than on an item, a small circle appears with a blinking cursor above it. Tap this circle with your finger and drag it around an item to literally lasso and select it. As when selecting with the pen, a dotted line appears around the selection. Depending on the item you select, a relevant radial menu appears with which you can use to work with the item. You can press and hold on the highlighted, selected, item to summon the options bar at the bottom of the screen.

Adding Tags and Items

Adding items to notes typically involves the Page radial menu described earlier in the chapter. The following list shows you how to add the various types of items to your notes.

✔ **Adding tags:** You can add tags to virtually any item using pretty much any of the main menus, which all come with a Tags item. As with other elements, there are fewer tags than with OneNote 2013, but you do have eight to choose from: Clockwise from the top, they are Critical, Contact, Address, Phone Number, Remove Tags (this is grayed out if there are no tags to remove on the item), To Do, Important, and Question.

✔ **Adding tags:** You can add tags to virtually any item using any of the main menus that come with a Tags item. As with other elements, there are fewer tags than with OneNote 2013, but you do have eight to choose from: Clockwise from the top, they are Critical, Contact, Address, Phone Number, Remove Tags (this is grayed out if there are no tags to remove on the item), To Do, Important, and Question.

Whichever tag you choose becomes the tag shown as the item label on the menu.

✔ **Creating bullets and lists:** Most menus have the List item on it. Simply access this submenu to choose from four types of bulleted lists, a numbered list, or three types of outline-style lists, namely: i, ii, iii; A, B, C; and a, b, c.

✔ **Adding photos:** From the Page menu, you can access the Camera item or submenu. If you tap the Camera item the Camera app appears so you can shoot a picture, but if you tap through to the submenu, you can also choose the Picture item to add an existing photo.

✔ **Inserting and customizing tables:** Select the Table item on the Page menu to insert a two-cell table to your note page. Then select the Table button to access the Table menu, and you see table-related options that allow you to add rows, columns, lists, tags, and pictures or to change the sorting order of the table. The Sorting Order submenu has a Header Row menu you can use to create a row at the top of the table where you can toggle between sorting or not sorting the top row.

You can tell whether the Header Row item is toggled on or off by checking for a dark purple outline inside the outer pink circle; if it's there, your header row is on, if it's not there, your header row is off.

Formatting Notes

The process of formatting notes in OneNote for Windows 8 is a little different than it is in OneNote 2013 — okay, it's *way* different. The following sections describe how to perform the major formatting tasks in OneNote for Windows 8.

Modifying and manipulating text

Because OneNote for Windows 8 has no Ribbon, you work with text a little differently than you do in other apps, namely via the Text radial menu. Selecting text summons the menu's button, which you can click or tap to view the typical options for formatting your text. Note that the appearance of some items on the menu is a little misleading; more's there than meets the eye, as I show in the following list. From the top item, moving clockwise around the menu are the following main items:

✔ **Font color:** Choosing this item results, quite frankly, in a very cool-looking submenu that allows you to select your font color from a spectrum, as shown in Figure 6-5. Simply tap or click the Font Color item, choose a color submenu item, and select an item from the resulting submenu. Choose black and you see a submenu with multiple versions of gray, including black and white; choose red and you see multiple versions of red, such as pink; and so forth.

Figure 6-5: Pick a color — any color!

To the left of the Font Color item on the Font Color submenu (this item does nothing when you tap or click it) are the Fill item to the left and the Highlight item to the right. Choose the Fill item (it's grayed out unless you're in a table cell) to fill a table cell with a color, and choose the Highlight item to see and select highlighter colors.

The Highlight option here is the only method to highlight anything in OneNote for Windows 8 as of this writing. Although you do have up to four custom pens available to you, none of them can be highlighters. This limitation is certain to change in the future. In the meantime, you can highlight text much like you can in Microsoft Word: simply select text and choose from the highlighter colors on the Text radial menu to apply the highlighter color to the selected text.

✔ **Font:** This menu is literally just a list of four fonts with a More link that loads up an extensive list of other available fonts.

✔ **Bold:** Although the submenu item here shows Bold, which may lead you to believe the submenu is all about bolding text, this submenu is in fact a text-formatting menu with bold, italic, subscript, strikethrough, and similar text-formatting options.

✔ **List:** Here you find a few of the more popular bullet list types to turn the selected item into a bullet. As is standard with the app, there aren't nearly as many choices as there are in OneNote 2013.

✔ **Copy:** Select this item to see Copy, Paste, and Cut items on the submenu.

✔ **Tag:** Choose here from the more popular tag types described in the next section.

✔ **Undo:** In addition to Undo, you also see Redo, which will be grayed out if you have nothing to redo. If you tap Redo, it will gray out, and the Undo item will become accessible indicating you can undo what you just redid. The Clear Format item also allows you to remove formatting from the current selection.

✔ **Font size:** This submenu is really a radial dial with the smaller font sizes at the upper left and the larger sizes at the lower left; tap and hold or click and then drag clockwise to increase font size; drag counterclockwise to decrease size.

Adding or removing lines

By default, note pages are blank, white pages, but if you prefer some background lines, you can easily have them. Although OneNote for Windows 8 doesn't have nearly the options for page backgrounds that OneNote 2013 does, it does have two very important options: graph paper and ruled paper.

To add lines to your page, access the options bar by right-clicking or swiping up from the bottom of the screen, selecting the Paper button, and choosing either Show Rule Lines or Show Grid Lines.

To remove lines, access the Paper button by right-clicking anywhere on the screen or swiping up from the bottom of the screen; then choose Hide Lines. Note that you cannot have both rule lines *and* grid lines.

Changing a section's color

To change the color of a section, press and hold on or right-click the name of the section and tap the Section Color button that appears in the bar at the bottom of the screen. You have 16 colors to choose from.

Writing and Erasing Ink

Surface Pro and functionally equivalent PCs come with a Wacom digital pen, as described in Chapter 1, with which you can write on the screen of your PC.

 Because the Surface Pro is the first Windows 8 PC to include the pen and is essentially a reference for other PC makers — not to mention that I own one — that device is what this chapter is written with. If you have a different device, your mileage may vary.

 You can use ink technologies only on PCs built with the technology included, such as Surface Pro. Non-touchscreen PCs and the Microsoft Surface RT don't support this feature without help from external devices such as Wacom tablets.

Writing with the pen

Writing with a digital pen, such as the one that comes with Surface Pro, is as easy as writing on a piece of paper. Here's how to write on your Surface Pro (or other tablet that supports digital pen technology):

1. **Open up a new note in the OneNote for Windows 8 app.**

2. **Bring the tip of the pen to the surface of the Surface "or other digital-pen compatible PC."**

   As the pen nears the surface of the Surface Pro screen, a small hand symbol appears over the page where your pen's tip is and moves along with the tip of the pen. The Ink menu button also appears at the right side of the screen if you need it.

3. **Touch the pen to the screen's surface and drag it *very* lightly along the screen.**

   As you drag the pen lightly across the surface of the screen, you see your mark as a line of the thickness and color of whichever of your four favorite pens you're using, but the lighter you press the tip against the screen, the fainter the line is.

4. **Repeat Step 3, but press a bit harder this time.**

   Notice that the line darkens.

   Don't press too hard! The darkness of the line increases only so much, and you don't want to break the tip of the pen or scratch the surface of your device.

Erasing with the pen

On the reverse side of the Surface Pro digital pen is what looks suspiciously like an eraser. Guess what? It is an eraser. To erase ink, and only ink — you can't erase symbols, bullets, links, photos, or anything except ink — simply turn the pen around, touch the eraser end to the surface of your screen, and wipe away your ink. It's that simple.

Unlike with OneNote 2013, which has three thicknesses of erasers and a Stroke Eraser, the only eraser you get with OneNote for Windows 8 is a little thicker than OneNote 2013's Small Eraser but not as thick as that app's Medium Eraser. It is perhaps half the width of the eraser end of the digital pen itself. Microsoft is likely to add more eraser options in the future.

Managing Your Notes

Managing notebooks, sections, and notes is mostly done via the options bar that appears when you right-click or press and hold on a portion of the screen. The following list shows you how to perform the major tasks:

✓ **Add a notebook, section, or page.** As you look at the default interface, notice the + symbol in a circle above every column; from left to right you see +Notebook, +Section, and +Page (refer to Figure 6-1). Tap one of these to create a new notebook, section, or page, respectively. You can also tap the New Page item on the options bar to add a page to the current section while editing a note page.

✓ **Rename a note page.** Click or tap in its title portion at the upper left and replace the title (if any) with a new one. Whatever you enter into the title field appears as the name in the Pages column.

✓ **Rename a section or notebook.** To rename a section, right-click or press and hold on the current name of the section in the Section column and select the Rename Section button. Select the highlighted text and use the keyboard that appears to type a new name; then tap anywhere outside the field to confirm the name.

✓ **Copy a link to a notebook, section, or page.** You can copy a link to a section by right-clicking your mouse or pressing and holding on a notebook, section, or page name and tapping or clicking the Copy Link To option. The link is then copied to your Clipboard for you to paste where you will.

With links you can e-mail notes or share them via instant messaging or even social networks.

✔ **Pin a section or page to the Start screen.** You can right-click or press and hold on a section or page name and choose Pin to Start to pin the item to the Start screen for easy access. For whatever reason, you can't do this with a notebook.

✔ **Make a page a subpage.** Right-click or press and hold on a page name and choose the Subpages menu; from here, you can choose Make Subpage to (yes) make the page a subpage, or, if it's already a subpage, choose Promote Subpage to promote a second-level subpage to a regular subpage or to promote a regular subpage to a regular page.

You can have up to two levels of subpages. If a page is not a subpage, the Promote Subpage item will be grayed out; if a subpage is a second-level subpage, the Make Subpage item will be grayed out.

Chapter 7

Taking Notes on Android Devices

· ·

In This Chapter

▶ Checking out the OneNote Android interface

▶ Taking notes and adding photos

▶ Managing your notes . . . or not

· ·

*O*neNote for Android is the baby of the OneNote mobile apps — the most recent, that is, as well as the least functional in most ways. One of the ways this is most evident is the fact that the app has not been optimized for a tablet experience at all. As a result, instructions for the smartphone are identical to instructions for using the app on a tablet.

In this chapter, I show you how to use the Android version of OneNote to take notes, sync notes to SkyDrive, and more.

Navigating the Interface

OneNote on Android sports a very stripped down interface that is designed first and foremost for smartphones, and it really looks and works a great deal like the Windows Phone version of the app, as shown in Figure 7-1.

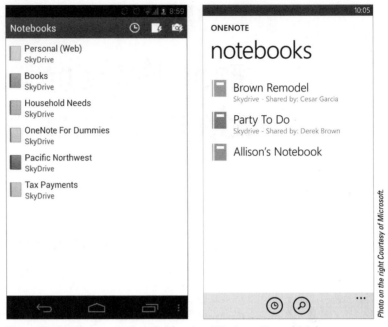

Figure 7-1: OneNote on Android (left) and on Windows Phone (right).

Because Windows Phone has such a small market share, I don't discuss it in detail in this book. However, in terms of functionality, its use is closer to that of the Android version of OneNote than to the iOS version.

Just like the Windows Phone OneNote interface, OneNote for Android is extremely utilitarian to behold; this is especially obvious on an Android tablet, in which the interface is identical to a smartphone interface but with a whole lot of space interspersed between all of the screen elements, as shown in Figure 7-2.

The major elements of the OneNote for Android user interface are as follows:

✔ **Note pane:** The note pane takes up the entire screen except for the top strip where the buttons reside.

✔ **Up button:** This up-arrow button appears in the upper-left corner of the OneNote interface whenever you're anywhere but the Home screen. Tap it or even the name of the page — it's really all one big button — and you'll go back to the section, note, or list that you were looking at previously.

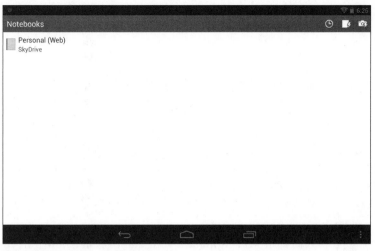

Figure 7-2: Android on a Nexus 7.

✔ **Command buttons:** At the top of the screen to the right of the up-arrow button are three buttons that let you perform important functions in the app. You see these buttons while working anywhere in OneNote except the Home screen; they are as follows:

- *Recent Notes button:* The left-most buttons in the upper-right corner of the app lets you access recent notes.

- *New Note button:* The middle button is the New Section button. Tap this, and a new blank note appears with your cursor in the title field. See the "Creating a new note" section later in this chapter for more information on creating a new note.

- *Take Picture button:* The right-most button at the top of the window lets you snap a photo to add to your note. See the "Adding a picture to a note" section later in this chapter for more information.

✔ **Keyboard:** If you tap any note so that your cursor is in the note, your device's keyboard appears just as it does in any Android app.

Writing Notes

As with other mobile versions of OneNote, such as the iOS and Web App versions, the Android version of OneNote allows you to access and edit notes with a minimal feature set in comparison to desktop versions of OneNote, such as OneNote 2013. The following sections get you up to speed on note taking with OneNote Mobile on Android devices.

Creating a new note

You can create a new note no matter where you are in OneNote, whether you're viewing a page, section, or your list of notebooks by tapping the middle button in the upper-right corner of the OneNote interface — it looks like a piece of paper with a lightning bolt on it. If you're in a section or viewing a note, the new note appears in that section; if you're at the Home screen, the new note appears instead in the Unfiled Notes section of the Personal (Web) notebook.

This icon won't appear if your cursor is in a note; tap your device's Back button to restore the New Note icon.

Opening existing notes

You can open an existing note from OneNote by tapping its name while viewing the section it resides in. To do so, from the Home screen, simply tap the name of the notebook the note is in, tap the name of the section it's in, and then tap the name of the note.

Adding list elements to notes

List elements in OneNote for Android are hidden until you need them. To access them, tap into a note, and the buttons at the top of the screen will change. From left to right, the buttons include the Camera button, which allows you to add photos to a note, and the three list element buttons, which from left to right are for numbered lists, bulleted lists, and check boxes. Tap any of these three items to add a number, bullet, or check box, respectively, to an existing or blank item.

Recording notes

If you're on the run and want to speak your note to OneNote instead of typing it, you can. OneNote will take your recorded words and translate them into text characters in your currently open note. You can talk to OneNote using one of the more prevalent buttons in the Android interface: the microphone button, which is included on the keyboard and has an icon of an old-style microphone on it.

Follow these steps to speak a note into a note:

1. **Open an existing or new note and tap the note pane where you would ordinarily type.**

   The Android keyboard appears.

2. **Tap the microphone button on the keyboard.**

   The Speak Now screen appears onscreen, as shown in Figure 7-3.

Language drop-down menu

Figure 7-3: Speaking to OneNote.

3. **Speak your text into the device's microphone.**

   OneNote interprets your speech and adds its interpretation as text in the note, and the Speak Now text changes to say "Tap to Pause," as shown in Figure 7-4.

   If you don't start speaking immediately or stop speaking for an extended period of time, a keyboard icon appears at left, and the words "Tap to Pause" change to "Tap to Speak." Tap the big circle on the screen and then start speaking.

4. **Tap the bottom portion of the screen (where it says "Tap to Pause") while speaking to pause speech recognition.**

Figure 7-4: Tap to pause speaking.

You can either tap the screen again to continue speaking where you left off or tap the keyboard icon to switch back to the keyboard if you're done speaking and want to edit the text. You can also simply tap the device's Back button to hide the keyboard and make the note full-screen again.

A language drop-down list appears at the top of the Speak screen — it shows your default language, such as "English US" — here you can either choose another language or add another language if you haven't done so yet.

Adding a picture to a note

You can add existing pictures to your note or snap an image for the note as long as your device has a camera — as most Android devices do. You have two choices when adding a picture to a note:

✔ **Take Photo button:** As I mentioned earlier, when you're any-where except in an actual note, you see a camera icon with a lightning bolt on it in the upper-right corner of the interface. Tapping this icon allows you to snap a shot for the note you're currently viewing (see the next section for more information).

   If you tap this icon while in any notebook, OneNote auto-matically creates a note called Unfiled Note in your Personal (Web) notebook under the Unfiled Notes section; the new image will appear in this note.

✔ **Photos button:** This icon appears when your cursor is in the note. When this is the case, the buttons at the top of the screen change, and the top-left button becomes a camera. Tap this button, and a pop-up window appears where you can choose to add a photo from your gallery or to take a new photo.

Taking a new photo

Taking a new photo and adding it to your note are easy, especially if you're already familiar with your phone's camera.

OneNote doesn't have its own camera; it simply "borrows" the camera Android is set to use. The features of your camera depend on the version of Android you're using. The app doesn't support more advanced camera modes such as panorama or Google's Photo Sphere as of this writing; it supports only snapshots. Similarly, OneNote doesn't support capturing and adding video.

Follow these steps to snap a new photo to include in your note page:

1. **Tap a note pane to edit it, if you're not already there, and then tap the camera icon at the upper left of the screen.**

   The Insert menu appears providing options to add an image from your gallery or capture a photo.

2. **Tap Capture a Photo.**

   The default Android camera appears. You see the standard camera options for your version of the Android camera; Figure 7-5 shows the camera for Android 4.2 (the second release of what Google nicknames the "Jelly Bean" version of the Android operating system).

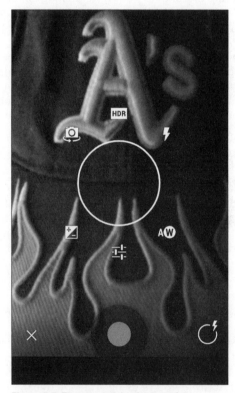

Figure 7-5: The camera for Android 4.2.

An X appears in the lower left of the screen, which you can tap to cancel if you decide not to take a photo after all. A circle representing the camera's options appears in the lower right. Tap this circle to control your camera's options, such as flash, exposure, and so on.

Although I don't have room in this book to teach you how to use your phone's camera — especially because options differ dramatically between cameras and versions of Android — it's worth noting that Figure 7-5 shows the Android 4.2 camera's radial menu interface because OneNote for Windows 8 also uses radial menus. See Chapter 6 for more information on radial menus.

3. **Snap a photo as you normally do.**

   The X symbol remains, but a check mark symbol replaces the options circle at the lower right.

4. **Tap the X if you don't like the picture and want to retake it; tap the check mark when you're satisfied with the photo.**

   Your note reappears with the photo in it.

Adding an existing photo

If you want to add a photo that you've already taken to your note, you can add it from your Android photo gallery. Here's how:

1. **Tap a note pane to edit it, if you're not already there, and then tap the camera icon at the upper-left of the screen.**

   The Insert menu appears with options to add a picture from your gallery or capture a photo.

2. **Tap Image from Gallery.**

   If SkyDrive or other apps are also installed, the first time you do this procedure, Android will present an overlay window asking which source you want to choose from. In this case, go to Step 3. If this doesn't appear, go to Step 4.

3. **Tap Gallery, SkyDrive, or another source and then tap Always or Just Once.**

   Your Android gallery or other source appears. If you chose Just Once, you will be asked again the next time you want to add an image. If you chose Always, OneNote will default to that source from now on.

   To undo this later, tap the Clear Data button by selecting OneNote under Apps in Android Settings.

4. **Tap among the various gallery folders to find the image you want to add.**

The image is added to the note.

Deleting notes

You can delete notes in the OneNote Mobile app, but you can't delete anything else without using the SkyDrive app, the Web App, or the desktop version of OneNote (see the next section).

To delete a note page, with the page open, tap the More Options button in the lower-right corner of the screen (it looks like three vertical dots) and then tap Delete Page.

Managing Notebooks and Notes

You really can't manage your notebooks, sections, or note pages in OneNote on Android. You can delete a note page by tapping the Delete Page button on the Options pane while viewing a note (see the previous section). However, you must handle procedures such as renaming, deleting, and moving sections or notebooks in the SkyDrive app or Web App version of OneNote (see Chapters 5 and 9, respectively, for more information on the Android SkyDrive app and the Web App version of OneNote).

To rename or delete a section or notebook, you must use OneNote Web App version or OneNote 2013, as discussed in Chapters 9 and 2, respectively, because none of the mobile apps for Android allow you to do so.

Checking Out OneNote Settings

OneNote Mobile for Android allows you to change very few settings in its Settings menu, and you can change a few items in other parts of the interface. The following sections get you up to speed on the settings available in the app as well as in the Android Settings menu.

Viewing the Options pane

OneNote organizes its settings by using a context-sensitive Options pane. You access this pane (see Figure 7-6) by tapping the button in the lower-right corner of the interface (the button consists of three vertical box-shaped dots). The buttons on the pane change slightly depending on where you are in the interface.

Figure 7-6: The Options pane in OneNote Mobile.

✔ While you're on the Home screen or in a notebook viewing sections, you see that the Options pane shows three buttons, including Sync, Sync Error, and Settings.

✔ While you're in a section viewing the pages, the pane also shows the New Page button.

✔ When you're viewing a note, note that the fourth button is the Delete Page button rather than the New Page button.

The buttons' purposes are as follows:

✔ **Sync:** Syncs the current page immediately.

✔ **Sync Error:** If you ever see the Sync Error icon in your notification bar, tap this button to get more information about the error.

✔ **Settings:** The various settings — mostly information, actually — are displayed here; see the next section for more info.

✔ **New Page:** Creates a new page within the current section.

✔ **Delete Page:** Deletes the current page.

Viewing the Settings menu

To access the main Settings menu, tap the Settings menu on the options pane while in any part of the OneNote interface (see the previous section). The top portion of the Settings menu is shown in Figure 7-7.

The Settings menu contains the following items:

✔ **Sync on Wi-Fi Only:** Tapping this check box prevents your device from syncing unless you're on a Wi-Fi connection, allowing you to conserve your data plan.

✔ **Windows Live ID Account:** Tap this item to view the Windows Live account you're logged in to. The screen you're taken to is actually in the Android settings app, not in OneNote. You see an options button in the upper-right corner (three square-shaped dots in a vertical line) that you can tap to access Sync Now or Remove Account and a Help option that opens your browser and loads help documentation about your device.

✔ **Upgrade:** OneNote Mobile is free for up to 500 notes, after which it allows you only to view, not edit, notes unless you delete some. Tap this item to visit the Google Play store and pay $4.99 to have unlimited notes.

✔ **Help:** Tap this item to summon your default browser and load Microsoft's online Help documentation for OneNote Mobile.

✔ **Support:** This item brings up your default web browser and loads support forums for the app.

✔ **Use Terms:** A pop-up window appears when you tap this item, showing the app's terms of use.

✔ **Privacy Statement:** Tap this item to bring up your default browser and view Microsoft's privacy statement.

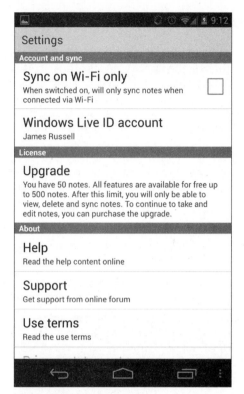

Figure 7-7: The Settings menu.

- ✔ **Third Party Notice:** This item summons a pop-up window displaying information about third-party technologies included in OneNote Mobile.

- ✔ **Version:** This item simply displays the app's version number.

- ✔ **Copyright:** This item only displays the copyright language for OneNote Mobile.

 Unlike other versions of OneNote, including the iOS and desktop versions, there is no method of configuring the image size or quality — the Android version of the app uses full-scale images whether you like it or not.

Viewing Android app settings

OneNote for Android includes some settings in the device settings that aren't accessible via the app. To access those settings, tap the Settings icon on your device's home screen or apps list, tap Apps, and then tap OneNote in the Downloaded or All lists. At the top are various buttons and a check box, listed as follows, and below those, you see the permissions that you agreed to when you installed the app.

- ✔ **Force Stop:** This button allows you to close OneNote if it won't close any other way. All processes stop, period.

- ✔ **Uninstall:** Tap this button to uninstall the app.

- ✔ **Clear Data:** Tapping this button temporarily clears the data stored on your device by OneNote, but as soon as you log in again, the data will reappear.

- ✔ **Clear Cache:** If OneNote is misbehaving, you can try tapping this button after tapping Force Stop; afterward, restart the app.

- ✔ **Clear Defaults:** This button is completely grayed out as of the time of this writing and may be enabled in a future upgrade.

Chapter 8

Taking Notes on iOS Devices

● ●

In This Chapter

▶ Finding your way around the interface

▶ Taking notes

▶ Viewing and changing your settings

● ●

*A*pple's iOS devices include iPad, iPhone, and iPod touch and were the first non-Microsoft platforms to get OneNote. As a result, in terms of user interface and functionality, the iOS version of OneNote is further advanced than Android and even Windows Phone versions. That said, its functionality is dramatically reduced in comparison to the functionality of OneNote 2013 or even OneNote Web App.

In this chapter, I show you how to do what you can in the iOS version of OneNote, from navigating OneNote to note-taking to configuring settings.

Navigating OneNote for iOS

OneNote on iOS has a unique interface, one that's unlike any other version of OneNote. It has a lot of very cool features, animations, and stylization that Apple's platforms are famous for. The following sections explain how to interact with OneNote on your iOS device.

Checking out the OneNote interface

OneNote on iOS devices all have the same interface, although the iPad version looks dramatically different given its larger size. Figure 8-1 shows the iPad version of OneNote in landscape orientation.

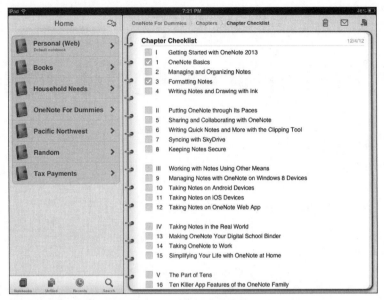

Figure 8-1: OneNote for iPad in landscape orientation.

The OneNote interface changes a bit in portrait orientation. As you can see in Figure 8-2, the navigation bar disappears, and the note pane takes up the entire screen. Look carefully and you'll notice a new icon in the upper-left corner of the screen; tap this icon to access the navigation bar and tap it again to hide it.

With iPhone and iPod touch, each pane takes up the entire screen, and the buttons and tabs are crowded together at the top and bottom of the screen.

Following are the major interface elements for the OneNote on iOS:

✓ **Note pane:** The note pane takes up the entire screen in portrait orientation and the right two-thirds of the screen in landscape orientation for the iPad version and looks like a piece of paper in a ring binder. For iPhone and iPod touch, each pane takes up the entire screen similar to portrait mode on iPad, but smaller.

Above the note pane, you see your current location in the format Notebook Name > Section Name > Page Name. Tap the name of the notebook or section if you're on a page to instantly jump to that location. If you want to view the notebook's sections, for example, tap the notebook name; if you want to jump back to viewing the list of pages within a section, tap the name of the section.

Figure 8-2: OneNote for iPad in portrait orientation.

✔ **List pane:** This is where you view your list of notebooks, sections within a notebook, or pages within a section. Tap an item and you see it sort of shimmy up to the top of the list.

On the Recents tab, tap the pin icon at the right of any item to pin it to the top of the list. It remains at the top of the list no matter what item you touch. Pin another item, and it goes below the first pinned item. Tap an item, and it appears below all pinned items.

✔ **Back button:** This button appears in the upper-left corner of the OneNote interface, except when you're on the Home page, which is the main interface where you view notebooks. The button looks like a left-facing arrow, and if you tap it you'll go back to the section, note, or list that you were looking at previously.

The text of this button changes depending on where you are and where you'll go back to if you tap the button. For example, if you're viewing a notebook's sections, the button displays Home. If you're viewing a section's pages, it displays the name of the notebook. No matter what the button displays, it's functionally a Back button.

✔ **New Section button:** At the top of the screen next to the Back button — anywhere in OneNote except the Home screen — is the New Section button.

✔ **Delete/E-Mail/New Page buttons:** In the upper-right corner of the app interface, you see buttons to delete, e-mail, and create notes.

✔ **View icons/Search button:** At the bottom of the window, you see three icons that you can tap to change the view of the list pane from notebooks to unfiled notes, recent notes, and the search view.

✔ **Keyboard:** If you tap any note pane, the keyboard appears, as shown in Figure 8-3.

The keyboard has its own elements, including the following:

• **Check box button:** Tap this icon to add a check box to the currently selected item (the item where your cursor appears in the note pane).

• **Bullet button:** Select this icon to add a bullet to the currently selected item.

You can add both a check box and a bullet to an item, but that looks a little funky.

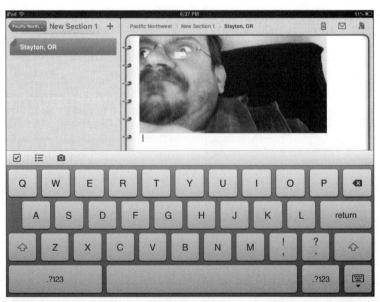

Figure 8-3: The OneNote onscreen keyboard.

- **Camera button:** Use the camera button to take or add pictures to a note. See the "Adding a picture to a note" section later in this chapter for more information.

- **Return button:** This button changes text depending on where you are in OneNote. If you tap the Search button and tap into the Search field, the button displays Search instead of Return. If you're signing in to the app, it displays Sign In instead.

- **Close keyboard button:** Tap this button to close the keyboard.

Writing Notes

Writing notes is easy in OneNote for iOS devices. Many functions are available, although the Web App version of OneNote and the full OneNote 2013 app have much more functionality. The following sections describe the functions that are available on the iOS version of OneNote.

Creating a new note

You can create a new note no matter where you are in OneNote, whether you're viewing a page, a section, or your list of notebooks. Here's how:

1. **Tap the New Note icon in the upper-right corner of the OneNote window.**

   A pop-up menu appears with two choices.

2. **Choose Create Note (Unfiled) or Create Note in Current Section depending on where you want the new note.**

   The first choice files the note in your Personal (Web) notebook under Unfiled Notes. The second choice creates a new note in the section listed at the top of the OneNote window, no matter where you are in the OneNote interface.

   If you happen to actually be in the Personal (web) notebook in the Unfiled Notes section, the second choice is grayed out because it's redundant.

   After you make your choice, your new note appears as Untitled Page in the relevant section; to edit it, just tap it in the list pane.

Opening existing notes

Opening an existing note from SkyDrive is not complicated. From the Home screen, simply tap the name of the notebook it's in, tap the name of the section it's in, and then tap the name of the note to open it.

Adding a picture to a note

When you tap a note pane so that your cursor is in it, a keyboard interface appears (refer to Figure 8-3). At the upper left of the keyboard is a camera icon. Tap this icon to bring up two choices: Camera and Photo Library. The following sections show you how to use each.

✔ **Camera:** Tap this item to summon the camera, with which you can take a new photo to add to your note. The camera screen is straightforward. It has a camera icon at the bottom that you tap to take a picture and a reverse camera icon at the upper-right that you tap to switch from front to rear camera.

After you snap a shot, you see two buttons at the bottom of the screen. The left button allows you to retake the photo if you're not happy with it, and the right button lets you use the photo if you're satisfied with it.

✔ **Photo Library:** Select this item to choose an existing image from your device's Photo Library.

If your iPad has no camera, you'll see Saved Pictures and Photo Stream as options instead.

Naming and renaming a note

After creating a new note, simply type its name above the heading line at the top of the note. When you tap out of the heading area, the name appears in the note's title in the list at the left. Replace an existing title to rename the note.

What you can't rename or add

If you want to rename a section or notebook using OneNote for iOS, well, you just can't. If you want to create a new notebook, well, you can't do that, either. You can, however, rename sections or note pages or add new notebooks using OneNote 2013 or OneNote Web App, as discussed in Chapters 1 and 9, respectively. You can rename notebooks on SkyDrive using the SkyDrive iOS app, which I discuss in Chapter 5.

Deleting notes

You have two ways to delete notes in the iOS OneNote app, as shown here:

✔ In the list pane, swipe a note item to the left, and a red Delete button appears; tap it to delete the note.

✔ Tap the trash can icon at the top of the app interface; from the single-item menu that appears, tap Delete This Page.

Searching Notes

OneNote for iOS has a great search feature similar to that of OneNote 2013, allowing you to search all notes for a single term.

Because of the limited feature set of OneNote for iOS, you can search for only text characters. If you want to search for tags, for example, you must use OneNote 2013.

Here's how to search in OneNote for iOS:

1. **Tap the Search button at the bottom of the OneNote interface.**

   The list pane changes to include no items in the list and a search field at the top of the pane.

2. **Type a search term into the Search Notebooks field at the top of the list pane.**

   Results populate the list pane below the search field.

3. **Tap any item to jump to the note that it's in.**

   The list pane remains populated with the search matches, and the note associated with the tapped item appears in the note pane.

Managing Notebooks

You really can't manage your notebooks in OneNote on iOS. Processes such as renaming, deleting, and moving notebooks on SkyDrive — the only place you can easily store notes — must be done in the SkyDrive app for iOS. See Chapter 5 for more information about managing notes in SkyDrive.

Configuring OneNote Settings

OneNote for iOS doesn't have a lot of settings you can actually change. Tap the Settings button at the top of the Home screen to summon the Settings window, as shown in Figure 8-4.

Settings	
Account	jhrussell@outlook.com
Storage	
Photo Uploads	Resized >
Version	2.1
Privacy	>
Terms	>
Help Center	>
Sign Out	

Figure 8-4: The Settings window.

Viewing in-app settings

The following list briefly describes the items in this window:

- ✔ **Upgrade:** OneNote for iOS allows you to have up to 500 notes with full features of the app free; if you want more, you'll have to pay to upgrade the app.

- ✔ **Sync Now:** Tap this item to immediately sync all notes that are set to sync automatically (see the next section for more info).

- ✔ **Notebook Settings:** Tap this item to choose which notebooks to sync automatically and simultaneously decide which appear on the OneNote app Home screen.

- ✔ **Image Size:** Use this item to determine the size of images you add to notes.

- ✔ **Sign Out:** Tap this item to sign out of OneNote.

- ✔ **Help and Support:** This item leads to a window that provides links to help documentation and community support forums.

- ✔ **Terms of Service:** Tap this item to read OneNote's terms of service.

- ✔ **Privacy:** Tap here to read OneNote's privacy documentation.

Viewing other settings

OneNote for iOS includes some settings in the device settings that aren't accessible via the app. To access these settings, tap the Settings icon on your device's Home screen and tap the OneNote icon in the Settings pane at the left. The OneNote settings then appear at the right, and are as follows:

- ✔ **Sync on Wi-Fi Only:** If you have a limited amount of data to work with, you'll probably want to toggle this item to On so that you don't wind up going over your data limits.

- ✔ **Reset Application:** If you have sync or other errors that don't fix themselves by restarting OneNote, toggle to On and then restart OneNote to reset the app. You'll have to sign in to the app; this option automatically toggles itself to Off.

- ✔ **Version:** You can't change this "setting"; it simply lists the version of the app that's on your device.

Managing note syncing

You can set individual notes to sync automatically — or not to — as well as whether or not to appear on the Home screen. To do so, follow these steps:

1. **From the Home screen, tap the Settings button at the top of the OneNote interface.**

   To get to the Home screen, tap the Back button until you can't anymore.

2. **Tap Notebook Settings.**

   The Notebook Settings window appears, as shown in Figure 8-5.

3. **Tap the On slider next to a notebook to toggle it Off.**

   A notebook with an Off slider next to it won't appear on the Home screen or sync automatically.

4. **Tap the Settings button in the upper-left corner and then tap the Close button in the upper right of the window.**

You return to the Home screen with notebooks set to Off no longer visible and no longer automatically syncing to SkyDrive.

Configuring image settings

OneNote gives you quite a few options for image size. Here's how to change the default image size for photos and images added to notes:

1. **From the Home screen, tap the Settings button at the top of the OneNote interface.**

2. **Tap Image Size at the top of the window.**

   The Image Size window appears with five possible settings:

   • **Small:** This item sets images to .5 megapixels.

   • **Medium:** Sets images to 1 megapixel.

   • **Large:** Sets images to 2 megapixels.

   • **Actual Size:** Sets images to actual size.

   • **Ask Me:** Prompts you each time you add an image to decide what size to set it.

3. **Choose an item to select it and then tap the Settings button to return to the Settings window.**

Figure 8-5: The Notebook Settings window.

Chapter 9

Managing and Taking Notes with OneNote Web App

In This Chapter

▶ Getting used to the OneNote Web App interface

▶ Taking notes with OneNote Web App

▶ Searching notes

*O*neNote Web App is a stripped down version of the desktop version of OneNote. It includes the basic features of the desktop version and far more features than any of the mobile versions. OneNote Web App is mostly for those who don't own or currently have access to the desktop version and is the most fully featured free version of OneNote available. If you use OneNote on your mobile device, you can edit notes from any web-enabled device and manage notes in ways you can't with mobile versions of OneNote.

In this chapter, I show you how to create, edit, and manage notes via OneNote Web App.

Accessing the OneNote Web App

To access the OneNote Web App, you need at least a SkyDrive account. You also can access the Web App from an Outlook.com account, although you'll be accessing the Web App via SkyDrive anyway, because Outlook.com comes bundled with the SkyDrive service.

You can access the OneNote Web App in one of several ways:

✔ Access a link in an e-mail that was sent to you by someone sharing a note with you.

✔ Open a notebook from an e-mail while logged in to Outlook.com.

✔ Select the notebook at SkyDrive.com and from the top bar, choose Open⇨In OneNote Web App.

✔ Visit SkyDrive.com and at the upper left of the page, choose Create⇨OneNote Notebook.

Exploring the OneNote Web App Interface

When the note opens in the OneNote Web App, the interface resembles the desktop version, as shown in Figure 9-1.

The major parts of the interface are as follows:

✔ **Tabs and Ribbon:** The familiar Office tabs and Ribbon, as well as the commands on the Ribbon, are at the top of the page. At the upper right of the screen, you see the name of the account that you're logged in to on SkyDrive.com as well as Sign Out, Help (the question mark), Feedback (the weird box-like icon), and Exit (the large X) buttons. Below those, you see a down arrow that you can use to either hide or show Ribbon commands.

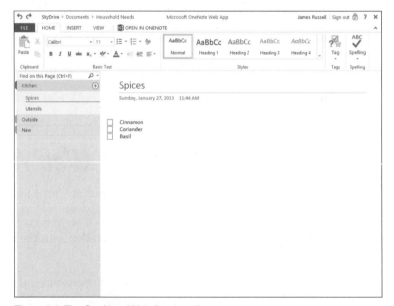

Figure 9-1: The OneNote Web App interface.

✔ **List pane:** The sidebar at the left shows sections and notes, and it changes according to what you're viewing (Figure 9-1 shows sections). Note also the Search field at the top of the sidebar.

✔ **Note pane:** This pane is at the right, just as it is in the OneNote desktop version, and displays the currently open note.

Getting familiar with tabs

The OneNote Web App has four tabs on its main interface and a reading mode with a slightly different interface. The tabs are described in the following sections.

File

The File tab reveals a pane that looks like the File tab in OneNote 2013 but has fewer options. Figure 9-2 shows the File tab's pane.

The following items are listed on the pane at the left:

✔ **Back button:** Tap the left-facing arrow to get back to your note.

✔ **Info:** This item simply contains a link to open the note in the desktop version of OneNote.

✔ **Share:** Access this item to e-mail a note to someone, to grab a link to post or even text someone, or to post the note to Facebook, Twitter, or LinkedIn.

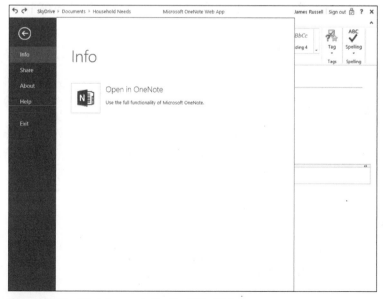

Figure 9-2: The File tab pane in the OneNote Web App.

✔ **About:** Here you can see a link to a trial version of Office, read the app's terms of use, or view information about privacy and cookies.

✔ **Help:** Find links here to online help documentation and to give feedback to Microsoft.

✔ **Exit:** Select this item to close the OneNote Web App.

Home

The Home tab (refer to Figure 9-1) is very similar to the Home tab in OneNote 2013, though with fewer features included. Refer to Chapter 3 for more information on the OneNote 2013 Home tab.

Insert

Use the Insert tab, shown in Figure 9-3, to insert photos, clip art, tables, and links or to create a new page or section.

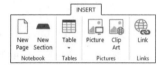

Figure 9-3: The OneNote Web App Insert tab.

View

The View tab, shown in Figure 9-4, has just a few options on it related to the information that's displayed on the page and the sidebar at left.

✔ **Editing View:** This view is the default that allows you to edit notes.

✔ **Reading View:** This view is essentially a stripped-down version of the interface that makes reading easier and totally disables editing. See the next section for more information on this view.

You can enable only one of these two views at a time.

✔ **Show Authors:** When selected, this item shows the user who created each page.

✔ **Page Versions:** Select this item to display versions of pages on the bar at left.

Figure 9-4: The OneNote Web App View tab.

Checking out the Reading View

The Reading View essentially doesn't allow editing of any kind. Most notable is the Ribbon, which changes a bit in Reading View as you can see in Figure 9-5.

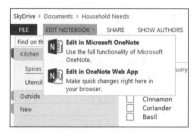

Figure 9-5: The modified Ribbon in Reading View.

To get into Reading View, select Reading View from the View tab. To get back to Editing View, choose Edit Notebook and then Edit in OneNote Web App. The tabs change significantly; in fact, they're no longer really even tabs because there are no Ribbon commands on them. The following list describes each of the Reading View's "tabs":

- ✔ **File:** This tab hasn't changed a bit from the version in Editing View (see the previous section).

- ✔ **Edit Notebook:** This is a drop-down menu with the option to open the note for editing in either the desktop version of OneNote or OneNote Web App.

- ✔ **Share:** This is the identical interface that you get when you choose Share from the File tab. Sharing is discussed briefly later in the chapter in "Sharing Notes" section and in more depth in Chapter 10.

- ✔ **Show Authors:** Choose whether to show authors' names while you're reading; this option is also on the View tab in Editing View.

Managing Your Notes

OneNote Web App is the catch-all *"if you can't do it in the mobile version, do it here"* solution for mobile OneNote users who don't own or currently have access to the desktop version of the app, which is by far the most functional version. The following sections bring you up to speed with the basics of managing your notes with OneNote Web App.

Making new notes

You can create a new note, section, or notebook easily in OneNote Web App. The following sections show you how.

Creating a new notebook

To create a new notebook for use in the OneNote Web App, you must be logged in to SkyDrive.com. Here's how:

1. **While logged in to SkyDrive.com, from the top of the screen, select Create⇨OneNote Notebook.**

   A pop-up menu appears with a text field and a default name for the selected notebook.

2. **Type a name for your notebook and then click or tap Create.**

   Your new notebook appears in the OneNote Web App.

Creating a new section

To create a new section, select the Insert tab and click or tap the New Section button. The new section will be named Untitled Section; you can rename it as you wish, as I describe later in the section "Renaming notes."

You can also right-click or press and hold the name of the section above the one you want to add and choose New Section from the context menu. The new section will be created below the first section.

Creating a new note

To create a new note page, click or tap the plus symbol to the right of the section name you want the note to fall under in the bar at the left. The new page will be named Untitled Page; you can rename it as you wish, as describe in the section "Renaming notes" section later in this chapter.

You can also right-click or press and hold the name of the section and choose New Page from the context menu.

Opening existing notes

Opening a notebook, section, or page is simple, but the process for doing so depends on which one you're opening — notebooks must be opened in the SkyDrive.com interface, whereas sections and pages must be opened in OneNote Web App. The following sections show you how to do both.

Opening a notebook

To use OneNote Web App to edit a note, you must open a notebook in the SkyDrive.com interface. Follow these steps to open a notebook:

1. **Log in to SkyDrive.com and navigate (if necessary) to the folder containing the notebook you want to open.**

   Your cursor turns into a hand, unless you're hovering over the check box in the upper-right corner.

2. **Click or tap the item.**

   The file opens in OneNote Web App.

 At the very top of the OneNote Web App interface you see a path showing you where you are. As shown earlier in Figure 9-1, the path is SkyDrive > Documents > Household Needs. Each item in the path is a link that you can click to return to the SkyDrive interface.

Opening a section or page

To open a section or page, select the name of the section you want to see while viewing the notebook containing the section or page. Similarly, with the section containing the chosen note open, just select the name of the page, and it opens in the pane at the right.

Adding formatting and tags

Working with formatting and tags in OneNote Web App is the same process as used in the desktop versions. Refer to Chapter 3 for information about note-taking basics. Some elements described there aren't in OneNote Web App, including styles, the Format Painter, and Outlook-related items.

Renaming notes

Unlike with the mobile versions of OneNote, in OneNote Web App, you can rename notebooks, sections, and notes. The following sections explain how.

Renaming a notebook

You must rename a notebook in the SkyDrive.com interface, as follows:

1. **Log in to SkyDrive.com and navigate (if necessary) to the folder containing the notebook you want to open.**

   Your cursor turns into a hand unless you're hovering over the check box in the upper-right corner.

2. **Click or tap to select the notebook and in choose Rename from the Manage menu at the top of the page.**

   You can also right-click or press and hold on the notebook and choose Rename from the context menu that appears.

   A field appears around the name of the notebook with the name selected.

3. **To rename the file, type the new name and then click or tap anywhere outside the field.**

Renaming a section or note page

Renaming a section or note page is straightforward, as shown here:

1. **Log in to SkyDrive.com and open the notebook containing the section or note page you want to open.**

   The notebook appears in OneNote Web App.

2. **Right-click or press and hold on the name of a section or note in the sidebar at left and choose Rename from the context menu.**

   A field appears around the name of the section or page with the name selected.

3. **To rename the section or page, type the new name and then click or tap anywhere outside the field.**

Deleting notes

You can delete notes in OneNote Web App, although the process differs slightly, depending on what you're deleting. The following sections discuss deleting notebooks, sections, and pages, as well as how to get a deleted notebook back from the SkyDrive Recycle Bin.

Deleting a notebook

You must delete a notebook in the SkyDrive.com interface, as shown here:

1. **Log in to SkyDrive.com and navigate (if necessary) to the folder containing the notebook you want to delete.**

   Your cursor turns into a hand, unless you're hovering over the check box in the upper-right corner.

   You can also right-click or press and hold on the notebook and choose Delete from the context menu that appears.

2. **Click or tap to select the notebook and choose Delete from the Manage menu at the top of the screen.**

The file is deleted and SkyDrive notifies you via a pop-up menu with an Undo button, which you can press if you don't want to delete the notebook after all.

Deleting sections or pages

You can quickly delete a section or page. Simply right-click or press and hold on the name of a section or page and choose Delete. OneNote Web App warns you that this action is irreversible. To delete the section or page, click or tap Yes.

Deleting a section deletes all pages in that section.

Salvaging deleted notebooks from SkyDrive's Recycle Bin

Although deleting sections and pages is final, deleting a notebook or any other file from SkyDrive.com puts that file into the Recycle Bin, which is accessible at the bottom of the left sidebar. To retrieve a previously deleted notebook, follow these steps:

1. **While logged in to SkyDrive.com, click or tap the Recycle Bin link near the bottom of the sidebar at left.**

   A list of your deleted files appears.

2. **Select the check box next to the notebook you want to restore and click or tap Restore at the top of the page.**

   You can also right-click or press and hold on a file and choose Restore.

   Your file is restored to the location it was in before you deleted it.

Changing section color

Section colors can be based on simple color preferences or to help you organize your notes; for example, you can use various shades of blue for all work-related notes and pink for all home-related notes. Whether you want to change the title bar color of a section purely for aesthetic purposes or for some organizational purpose, you can easily do so: Simply right-click or press and hold on a section title in the bar at left and choose a color from the Section Color submenu of the context menu that appears.

Creating subpages by indenting

You can create pages underneath a page, or *subpages,* and OneNote Web App supports indenting to help you do just that. You may want to do so, for example, if a page relates to all of the subpages and you want to keep them visually tied to the page. To indent a page, right-click or press and hold on a section title in the bar at left and choose Increase Indent. Choose Decrease Indent instead to move the page back to the left.

You can indent only twice, and you can indent only pages that have pages above them.

Sharing Notes

The OneNote Web App gives you quite a few options for sharing notes, including sharing via e-mail; via social networks such as Facebook, Twitter, and LinkedIn; and via links that you can post or share anywhere you want to. Because sharing is such a broad topic, I devoted Chapter 10 to it.

Linking to a Note

You can copy a link to a note so that you can share it with others and they can view it in their web browsers. To do so, right-click or press and hold on the name of a page in the bar at the left, choose Copy a Link to This Page, and copy the link that appears. You can then paste the link into an e-mail or anywhere you want, and anyone viewing it can access your page.

Getting a link in this fashion allows viewing only, and you can't shorten the URL. If you want to provide editing capabilities or shorten your URL, see Chapter 10 for information on sharing from SkyDrive.com.

Searching Your Notes

The OneNote Web App has a more limited search feature than the desktop version, which can search through an entire notebook and even through audio files for speech. However, for searching for text within sections or pages, the OneNoteWeb App search feature works just fine.

To search for a term, type it in the Find in this Page field, located at the top of the sidebar at the left side (refer to Figure 9-1) and press Enter or click or tap the magnifying glass icon. The arrow to the right of the Search box lets you choose whether to search just a page or an entire section.

Part III
Putting OneNote Through Its Paces

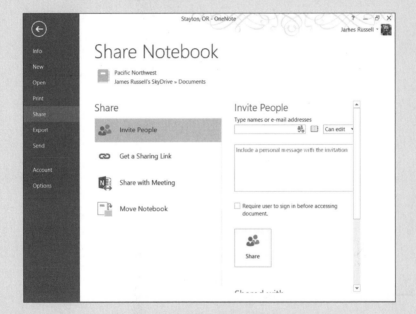

To learn how to turn OneNote 2013 into a digital coloring book, check out www.dummies.com/extras/onenote2013.

In this part . . .

✔ Get up to speed with sharing and collaborating on notes with others.

✔ Consider changing the way you take notes in class.

✔ Try taking notes in the workplace.

✔ Simplify your life with OneNote at home.

Chapter 10

Sharing and Collaborating with OneNote

In This Chapter

▶ Collaborating on notes with other users

▶ Sharing from Android or iOS

▶ Haggling with note permissions

▶ Sharing notes with others

*O*neNote was designed with sharing in mind. Indeed, Microsoft released OneNote on iOS and Android in addition to Windows Phone specifically to allow users to be able to share and access notes with anyone regardless of what smartphone or tablet device they had. The ability to share notes in this fashion with even non-Windows users such as those with Android and iOS devices is what makes OneNote of today so much more powerful than versions of the app from previous years.

In this chapter, I show you how to share your notes with people and collaborate on them no matter what version of OneNote you're using, how to view who changed what and when, and how to manage permissions on shared notes.

Taking Notes as a Team

You can invite multiple people to edit the same note at the same time, such as during a meeting, by housing the file on SkyDrive and sharing it. The following sections show you how to set up a notebook for viewing or editing by multiple people.

Sharing via OneNote 2013

To set up a notebook for use by multiple people and to invite them to it using OneNote 2013, follow these steps:

1. **Open the notebook you want to share with OneNote 2013.**

   The notebook you're sharing can't be a local computer that other users don't have access to. Advanced options such as SharePoint work much the same as SkyDrive, but the configuration options are outside the scope of this book.

2. **Select the File tab and choose Share.**

   The Share Notebook pane appears at the right, as shown in Figure 10-1.

3. **Choose from the following options:**

   • **Invite People:** Click this link to invite people by e-mail. You can allow recipients to view or view and edit the note via the drop-down box to the right of the field where you input e-mail addresses or names, but you must choose the same option for all of them. Lastly, you can add a personal message and select a check box if you want to require users to log in with a Microsoft account. (See the "Be kind: Warn people they'll need a Microsoft account" sidebar for more information on requiring log in.)

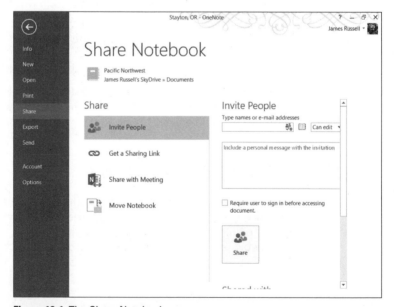

Figure 10-1: The Share Notebook pane.

Be kind: Warn people they'll need a Microsoft account

As this book's esteemed project editor Mark Enochs can attest from helping your author test the OneNote Web App sharing feature, setting up a Microsoft account isn't something to do when you're under pressure for time to do other meaningful things, like work. Microsoft wants quite a bit of information from you when you open an account, and you have to respond to its e-mails at least once to do so. Even then, its system is still being tweaked as of this writing and may not work properly.

If people need to log in to your note using a Microsoft account, give them some notice so that they can do so when they have some downtime; don't do so five minutes before a meeting where they'll be expected to have access to the note.

If you want to allow some people to edit and some people to just view a file, share first with one group and then share again with the other using the appropriate permission in the drop-down menu.

• **Get a Sharing Link:** Choose this option to get a link that you can share with others via whatever method you choose, be it by posting to a web page, using a social media network such as Facebook, using instant messaging, or posting a link on a web page.

If you want to enable editing only for certain participants and not others, share the Edit link with those you want to be able to edit the document and share the View link with those you don't want to be able to edit it.

One significant item that's present in OneNote Web App that isn't present here is the Share Via Facebook, LinkedIn, or Twitter item. You can still share via these networks by grabbing a link here and sharing it on the desired network.

• **Share with Meeting:** Select this option to share with an Outlook meeting. The meeting must be in process and must have note-sharing enabled. For more information, see *Outlook 2013 For Dummies* by Bill Dyszel.

• **Move Notebook:** This option leads only to a link that explains the logistics of moving notebooks that are already shared and how this can cause problems with syncing.

Sharing via OneNote Web App

OneNote Web App is the most functional version of OneNote aside from the desktop version, and sharing notebooks via OneNote Web App is similar, but not identical, to doing so via OneNote 2013. Some options in OneNote Web App just aren't in the desktop version of OneNote, as you'll see if you get familiar with both interfaces. Follow these steps to share a note via OneNote Web App:

1. **Open the notebook you want to share with OneNote 2013.**

   The notebook appears in your browser.

2. **Select the File tab and choose Share.**

   A nondescript white pane appears showing a solitary button named Share with People.

   When considering why Microsoft devoted an entire pane for a single button, your writer's first thought was that perhaps Microsoft was leaving the option open to add "Share with Cats" or "Share with Alien Beings" buttons in the future. His second thought, which perhaps makes more sense, is that for technical reasons, Microsoft didn't want to put the pop-up window's options on the pane and instead put the button on the pane to trigger the window. He still hopes his first thought is correct and that you will be able to share notes with cats or alien beings in the future.

3. **Click or tap the Share with People button.**

   A pop-up window appears, as shown in Figure 10-2, with multiple options for sharing.

   • **Send E-Mail:** Select this option to send a link to the note via e-mail. You can enter recipients in the To box and type a message, and you can choose to give editing access to recipients and require them to log in when accessing the note by selecting the appropriate check boxes.

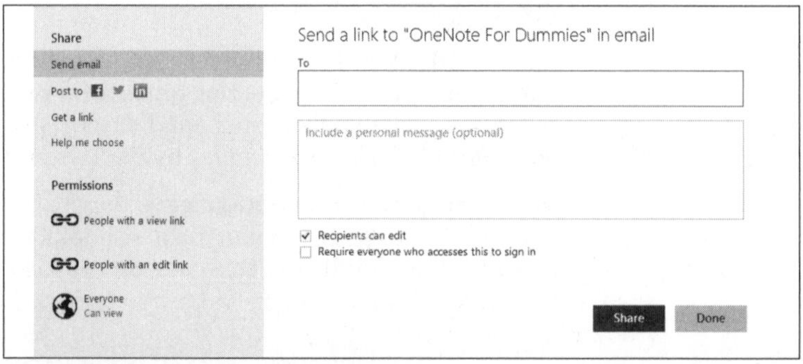

Share

Send email

Post to 🔲 ▾ 🔲

Get a link

Help me choose

Permissions

🔗 People with a view link

🔗 People with an edit link

🌐 Everyone
Can view

Send a link to "OneNote For Dummies" in email

To

Include a personal message (optional)

☑ Recipients can edit
☐ Require everyone who accesses this to sign in

Share   Done

Figure 10-2: Sharing in OneNote Web App.

- **Post To:** After you click the Post To item in the menu at left, you'll see a different set of options above the text box at right. Use this option to post the note to Facebook, Twitter, LinkedIn, or any combination of the three using the check boxes next to each network's icon. You can type a message to post with the link in the large text field below the symbols for the networks — if you've linked any networks (see the following Tip if you haven't). To allow those who click the link on your post to edit the file, select the Recipients Can Edit check box before posting.

Select Add Services to add services that aren't shown here. A drop-down menu will appear with other available networks listed and Find More Services and Manage Services links below. At the time of this writing, the only other service listed on the drop-down menu or at the Find More Services page is the Chinese Twitter-like network Sina Weibo. The Manage Services page lets you configure your current services.

- **Get a Link:** This option lets you choose one of three options: View Only, View and Edit, and Public. Click Create below the first two options to make read-only or editable links. Choose the Make Public button instead to make the file or folder searchable on the Internet and accessible to everyone.

This is the only place in the OneNote family of apps where you can see Microsoft's link shortener in action. When you click or tap one of the Create buttons, you'll see a Shorten item on the pop-up window that appears; click or tap that button to get a much shorter link to share.

The Public option isn't available in OneNote 2013 — perhaps because it involves sharing publicly from SkyDrive specifically and OneNote Web App is part of SkyDrive. Whatever the reason, this is the only place you'll see it.

- **Help Me Choose:** This option links to a website describing the preceding options in this list . . . and not much else.

Sharing via OneNote for Windows 8

At the time of this writing, sharing via the Windows 8 touch-enabled version of OneNote is a pretty limited affair — you can share via e-mail or choose to open the note in OneNote 2013 and share from that app, but that's it. To share from OneNote for Windows 8, follow these steps:

1. **Open the notebook to share in OneNote for Windows 8.**

   This version of OneNote can be opened only from the Start screen and can be used only with Windows 8.

2. **Access the Share charm.**

   The Share pane slides in from the right.

3. **Choose one of the following two options:**

   Mail: If you choose Mail, a pane appears showing a new e-mail in the Windows 8 Mail app already including the notebook as an attachment, as shown in Figure 10-3. If you haven't set up your Mail account yet, you'll first see a pane requesting your Microsoft account information.

   - **OneNote:** Choose this item to send the current page to the same notebook and section as a new page. A pane slides in from the right with which you can rename the new page if you like as well as a text field that you can use to add a note to the new page.

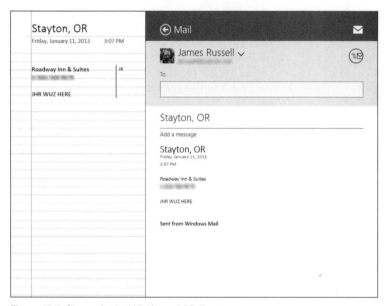

Figure 10-3: Share via the Windows 8 Mail app.

Sharing via mobile devices

As of this writing, sharing using OneNote apps for Android isn't possible. Sharing via iOS devices amounts to having a single e-mail button when you're viewing a page, which you can use to send the note to others. Otherwise, sharing via mobile devices is something you can do only with OneNote Web App, as discussed earlier in this chapter.

Sending Notes to Share Them

One of the simpler methods of sharing a note is by sending it as a file to an e-mail recipient or even to Microsoft Word or your blog. To send the current note as a file, follow these steps:

1. **Open the note you want to share in OneNote 2013 and select the File tab.**

2. **Click or tap Send and choose one of the following options:**

    - **E-Mail Page:** Choosing this item opens a new e-mail in your default desktop e-mail application with the current note page in web formatting either in the body of the e-mail or as a .mht attachment, depending on your e-mail program. The file won't be editable.

    - **Send as Attachment:** Select this option to attach a .one file (a OneNote 2013-2013 section file) to a new e-mail *and* to send the file in web formatting in the body of the e-mail and as a .mht attachment, depending on your e-mail program. The .one file is editable by recipients via whatever version of OneNote they have access to (at the very least OneNote Web App).

    - **Send as PDF:** Choose this item to send a PDF version of the currently open note page via e-mail.

     To send multiple pages, you must send each one as an individual PDF. If you want to do so, send each one to your e-mail address, save and name the PDF files as necessary, and then ZIP and send them all together, rather than bombarding recipients with a slew of individual PDF files.

    - **Send to Word:** Word has a lot more formatting capabilities than OneNote, and if you want to start a Word document from the currently open note page, choose this item. You can always send the file back to Word after you format it so that it looks nicer in OneNote.

    - **Send to Blog:** Selecting this item allows you to open the current page in Word's Web view so that you can format and post the current page using web formatting and then post it to your blog. Word will prompt you to register your blog, which you can either do immediately or the first time you post. The formatting is compatible with major blog formats such as Blogger, WordPress, and more.

Viewing Versions and Authors

Viewing versions of pages and authors can help you keep track of changes to documents as well as to who did what. Both OneNote 2013 and OneNote Web App allow you to view these things, but the controls for doing so are located in different places in each app's interface. The following sections describe how to view versions and authors in both apps.

Viewing versions and authors in OneNote 2013

You can view versions and authors in OneNote 2013 via the History tab, which is shown in Figure 10-4.

Figure 10-4: The History tab in OneNote 2013.

You have various options for viewing versions and authors:

- ✓ **Next Unread:** Move to the next unread change.

- ✓ **Mark as Read:** Here you can choose to mark a change as read or unread, mark the notebook as read or unread, or choose to show or hide changes in the notebook altogether.

- ✓ **Recent Edits:** From this menu, choose the time frame of changes you want to view. You can view changes as recent as today's changes or as far back as six months ago. The bottom option allows you to show all pages sorted by date.

- ✓ **Find by Author:** Access this item to show the Search Results sidebar at the right (see Figure 10-5). At the top is a search field with a drop-down menu next to it that allows you to change between searching the current section, section group, the entire notebook, or all notebooks. The drop-down menu below the search field allows you to sort results by date modified or author, and a button to the right that lets you choose whether to sort from A-Z (descending) or from Z-A (ascending).

- ✓ **Hide Authors:** Select this item, and author information will be hidden; select it again to show the information. When viewing authors, you can see the initials of individual contributors, as shown in Figure 10-6.

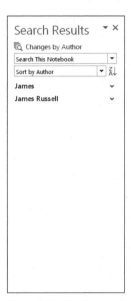

Figure 10-5: The Search Results sidebar.

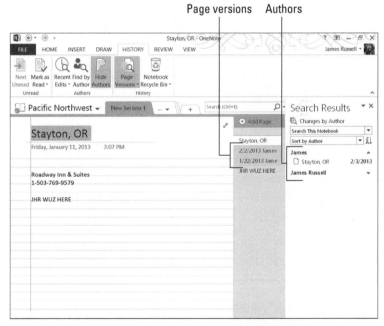

Figure 10-6: Viewing authors and version history in OneNote 2013.

Likely based on the assumption that you know what you wrote in OneNote 2013 (if you write in OneNote for Windows 8 your initials may be visible), your own information won't be displayed whether authors are hidden or not.

✓ **Page Versions:** This item lets you view all page versions, delete various configurations of page versions, or disable versioning history.

✓ **Notebook Recycle Bin:** Choose this item to show or hide the Notebook Recycle Bin as a read-only tab. Other options here allow you to empty the bin or to disable history altogether.

Viewing versions and authors in OneNote Web App

OneNote Web App has a much leaner set of options for viewing authors or versions than OneNote 2013; namely, it has one option for viewing each on the app's View tab:

✓ **Show Authors:** Select this button to show the names of authors of various changes next to the change itself, as shown in Figure 10-7. Select the button again to hide author names.

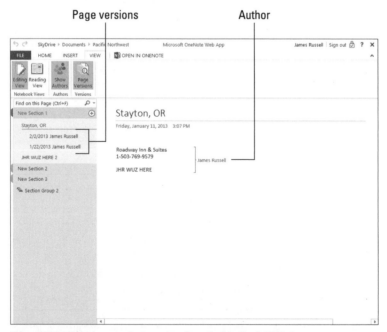

Figure 10-7: Showing versions and authors in OneNote Web App.

✔ **Page Versions:** Click or tap this button to show the versions of pages, as shown in Figure 10-7. Click or tap the button again to hide versions.

Managing Permissions

As with permissions for essentially any type of digital file or location, with OneNote, there are also two types: *view permissions* and *edit permissions*. The former lets people access and view the file; the latter lets people access, view, and change the file. Both OneNote 2013 and OneNote Web App place permissions and sharing options in the same place: in the Share options on the File tab. The following sections describe how to manage permissions in both apps, which is a similar, but not identical, process.

Managing permissions in OneNote 2013

You can change or remove permissions you give people to view or edit files using the Share option on the File tab in OneNote 2013 as follows:

1. **Open a notebook that is housed on SkyDrive.**

   If your note is housed elsewhere, your permissions options may differ or not exist at all.

2. **Select the File tab and then click or tap Share.**

   The Share Notebook pane appears at right.

3. **Right-click or press and hold on a permission under the Shared With section at the lower right of the pane.**

   A context menu appears.

4. **Choose the action desired from the context menu.**

   Actions shown will differ depending on what you're accessing:

   • **A user:** A context menu for a user shows a Remove User option, a Change Permission to View or Change Permission to Edit option depending on the permission, and contact links for that user.

   • **A shared link:** Context menus for links show Disable Link and Copy Link options.

   • **Social Networks:** This item states Everyone Can View or Everyone Can Edit; the context menu has Disable Posted Link and Change Permission to View or Change Permission to Edit options depending on the permission.

Removing permissions in OneNote Web App

OneNote allows you to give people both view and edit permissions; it also provides a third option — Public — that essentially gives anyone on the planet permissions to view (but not edit) the file. The "Sharing via OneNote Web App" section earlier in this chapter covers how to give these permissions; otherwise, you can only remove those permissions.

To remove permissions in OneNote Web App, follow these steps:

1. **Open the notebook for which you want to manage permissions in OneNote Web App.**

2. **Select the File tab, click or tap Share, and select the Share with People button.**

   A window appears with sharing options. Below these options are the permissions for the notebook, as shown in Figure 10-8.

3. **Select the permission you want to remove and choose Remove Permission.**

   There are a few other types of permissions with slightly different interfaces and options. For example, if you share a notebook on Facebook and then access the permissions for the notebook, you'll see a People on Facebook Can View or a People on Facebook Can Edit item that, when accessed, has a check box next to it that you can check or uncheck to add or remove editing permissions. You'll also see a Remove Permissions button to remove the permission altogether.

Figure 10-8: Viewing permissions in OneNote Web App.

Chapter 11

Taking Notes in the Real World

* *

In This Chapter

▶ Ogling how Surface Pro and OneNote transform computing

▶ Checking out OneNote as a study companion

▶ Adding OneNote to your workplace

▶ Taking OneNote home with you

* *

*T*he prevalence of smartphones and tablet computers is increasing (I can almost hear the whispers of boxes of new devices being opened), and with Microsoft finally blessing the iOS and Android operating systems with versions of OneNote, the app that started in Office 2003 is now coming into its own, helping to transform the way people work and live.

The good news is that you can use OneNote in all parts of your life, be it work, school, or home, and in this chapter, I show you how to do just that through examples that, though fictional, emulate real-world situations. No matter what your profession or what life throws at you on a daily basis, OneNote can help you handle it, and showing you how is the purpose of this chapter.

Approaching students on *their* terms

Students are most often young people, and no one tells young folks what phone or Internet device to use. With Office 2013, Microsoft has clearly figured this out, and OneNote is no longer relegated to Windows Phone. With OneNote for Android and iOS — or OneNote Web App for other Internet-capable devices — students can take notes no matter where they go or what phone or tablet they're using.

Oh, What a Difference a Day Makes!

Microsoft's Surface Pro and competing tablets with touchscreen, ink, and keyboard/mouse capabilities have completed the transitional period that began with smartphones and tablet computers such as Google's Android devices and Apple's iPad. Essentially, Surface Pro and competing devices are a PC in true tablet form, not tablets like Apple's iPad and Google's Nexus tablets are.

I'm writing this chapter on the day that Microsoft Surface Pro is being released, and for good reason. Until Surface Pro and similar devices by competing companies came along, multiple devices had to be used together in order to have the technologies required to take handwritten notes, snap photographs and video, type via a keyboard, and record audio. For the first time, Surface Pro puts those capabilities on one device that can run all legacy Windows software, and the result is a total overhaul of the personal computing paradigm.

In addition to reading this chapter, you can refer to Chapter 6, which I wrote using my new Surface Pro, to see just how different of a personal computing experience that Surface Pro — is bringing about.

There are two Surfaces; Surface Pro and Surface RT, the latter of which is related to Surface Pro only vaguely. It runs a version of Windows that doesn't support desktop apps for Windows 7 or prior versions of Windows. In regard to OneNote, however, with Surface RT, you still have access to a somewhat limited version of OneNote 2013, the Windows Store version of OneNote, and OneNote Web App, so really you're covered across the board for the discussion in this chapter.

Making OneNote Your Digital School Binder

OneNote is perfect for students; after all, who typically takes more notes than students? But OneNote is changing the nature of student note-taking: It allows you to include media that previously couldn't be part of note, such as the ability to search audio and video for terms, for example.

A brief OneNote history

The original OneNote was relegated to tablet PCs, which to some degree mirrored Microsoft's new Surface line but not to the degree necessary to fuel real adoption. Tablet PCs weren't really touchscreens in that you couldn't work with them via touch; they had pen and ink technologies in addition to running Windows software, and that was about all. Tablet PCs ran a superset version of Windows called Windows XP Tablet PC Edition, and at first it was the only edition of Windows that OneNote could run on. That situation changed with Office 2007, which for the first time broadened OneNote's appeal to regular Windows users, updated the interface to include the new Ribbon, and replaced Outlook in the Home & Student version of Office. Still OneNote was relegated only to Windows users on desktop PCs. As of this writing, even Office for Mac doesn't have OneNote, although it's rumored to be a part of Office for Mac 2014. Office 2010 upgraded OneNote's interface and file format in particular, but only in the Office 2013 cycle has OneNote received its wings with OneNote Web App and iOS, Android, and Windows Phone versions.

By contrast, back in the "Days of Yore" (2006) when I was last in college — yes, I walked barefoot to school in snow uphill both ways — I had a paper notebook that looked a lot like a teenager's room (read: a disaster) and a miniature cassette player to use for recording class lectures. That was it. Laptops were seen occasionally in class, but they were rare and frankly frowned upon by instructors because of the distracting "clickety clacking" sounds of typing (not to mention that the teachers assumed students were probably using the laptop to surf the web).

Today is different. Take Julie, a fictional student at Ye Olde High Tech University (YOHTU), which is of course encrusted in ivy, costs $5 short of a small fortune to attend per semester, and is located somewhere in New England. The following example shadows Julie during a typical day of classes to show how OneNote technology and its presence on multiple devices make her life different than life was for students "back in the day."

7:30 a.m.: Julie slings her lightweight backpack into her newfangled, sporty hybrid vehicle. Her backpack is light because her Surface Pro weighs only 2 pounds, and more importantly, because all her books are digital rentals from the university library stored on her Surface, she doesn't need to drag the hefty physical tomes to class with her. As a result, by the time she parks and walks the 18 miles from the parking lot of YOHTU to her classroom, she doesn't feel like her arm is going to fall off — although she does wish she had a spare pair of legs from all the walking she had to do to get to class.

8:25 a.m.: *Julie settles into her first class of the day — algebra. She whips out her Surface and moves the keyboard to the back side of the device because she doesn't need it right now. She moves her chair back a bit and sets the tablet on her lap with its pen device in hand; she brings up the Start screen and OneNote for Windows 8, and with a couple of swipes and a tap, accesses the algebra section of her fall semester 2014 notebook in OneNote, where she creates a new page under the section named after the day's date.*

8:32 a.m.: *Moments after class starts, the teacher begins presenting algebra equations, scribbling all over the white board like his arm is on crack. She watches nearly mesmerized as the board fills up in what seems like a minute and then realizes she hasn't written down half of the information. The teacher steps back from the board and gives the students a measly moment — the man doesn't seem to understand patience as a virtue — to finish transcribing what he's written on the board. Not panicking, Julie brings up her Start screen, taps to start her camera app, and uses the Surface Pro's front camera to snap a shot of the board. With a few taps, she drops the new image into the page she has open in OneNote. She quickly uses OneNote's Eraser tool to erase the few frenzied notes she wrote earlier, which are now redundant in light of the snapshot of the full whiteboard.*

11:30 a.m.: *Julie has lunch with some equally alegbra-fried girl-friends at the university cafeteria. She knows what she wants to order by the time she gets there because the university naturally has campus-wide Wi-Fi, and the daily menu and specials are posted on the campus web page. As they eat and chat, it turns out that neither of Julie's fellow students managed to scribble down the entire board, nor do they have a Surface Pro like Julie does. So, Julie whips out her Nexus phone — complete with Android Beam capabilities courtesy of the NFC chip inside — and her SkyDrive app. Julie and Ashley both happen to have OneNote Mobile for Android. Julie opens her phone and, simply by touching the two devices together and tapping Beam, she "beams" the page from her notebook to Ashley. Julie then pairs with her friend Jennifer's NFC-less iPhone via Bluetooth so that Jennifer can download the whiteboard image directly from Julie's phone.*

1:00 p.m.: *Julie's afternoon course is human anatomy, and today she and her classmates are lucky enough to get to dissect the gastrointestinal tract of a human cadaver. Before the instructor leads them to the "room with a view," as it were, Julie dons her face mask and grabs her Surface. A few minutes later, as the instructor pieces apart what used to be a human being, she uses her front-facing camera to record the entire "show" using OneNote's Record Video feature. The video is placed into the Anatomy section of her Fall Semester 2014 notebook on a page named after that day's date.*

7:30 p.m.: Julie goes home after class, eats the meager dinner of a full-time student, and then settles down at her desk to go over her notes for the day. She breaks out her Surface, separates the keyboard from the tablet, and sets both in front of her with the tablet's kick-stand back, essentially turning the device into a laptop form factor. Grabbing the HDMI cord from her 24-inch HD monitor, she plugs in to the tablet's mini HDMI port, and instantly her display from the tablet is extended onto the HD monitor. She opens OneNote 2013 rather than the Windows 8 version of the app — she prefers OneNote 2013's larger feature set for desktop use — and then retrieves her Bluetooth mouse from her backpack and turns it on.

Less than a minute after first sitting down, she is in front of a perfectly capable desktop system with an extended display on two monitors with which she can drag a window from one screen to the other. With the mouse, she first accesses the algebra page from earlier in the day. Seeing the screenshot of the board that she snapped, she right-clicks it and chooses Copy Text from Picture, opens a subpage for the cur-rent page, and pastes the text from the image into it. She names the subpage Whiteboard Text and translates the few equations that didn't translate properly using OneNote's equation tools.

*She then presses the E-Mail Page button on the Home tab of the OneNote Ribbon so she can e-mail the note page to her friend Jesse, who had asked her to e-mail today's class notes to him. A new e-mail window appears, and she drags it over to the Surface Pro's smaller screen because she prefers to keep OneNote 2013 open on the big monitor. She types **Here you go!** as the e-mail content, types his school e-mail address, types **Today's Algebra Notes** as the subject, and sends the e-mail. Jesse doesn't own OneNote, but he knows he can access her note via the OneNote Web App and find the important content there.*

Recalling then that she was too woozy during the extraction of the cadaver's stomach earlier in the day — there had been undigested "contents" in the cadaver's stomach — to recall the details she needed to for a group project, she goes back to OneNote on the HD monitor, clicks in the Search field, and searches for the word stomach. *OneNote searches through all her notes — including the audio from the video that she shot that day — and the results bring up the video set to the portion she's looking for. She plays back the video from that point, trying not to feel queasy again, and notices the details she couldn't recall earlier; she uses the keyboard to type the details on the note page right below where the video appears.*

When she's done studying — and quite honestly she's had enough of watching her teacher carve up a cadaver like a Thanksgiving turkey — she unplugs the HDMI cable from her Surface, closes the keyboard on the front of the device, closes the kickstand, and puts the device back into her backpack. She turns off the monitor, shuts off her desktop light, and goes to get ready for bed and start the whole process over the next day.

Just for clarity, the following list calls out the technologies and actions that made Julie's note-taking so efficient:

✔ Snapping shots of the board may have been possible on my phone back in 2005, but it certainly wouldn't have done much more good, other than to enable me to write the contents of the board onto paper. OneNote's OCR features allow text to be extracted from images and then edited and used wherever you need them in digital form without having to manually transcribe them. Granted, you need good lighting and legible words to extract text, but even the screenshot alone would have been more useful than her incomplete notes.

✔ OneNote can search notes for words even in audio and video files, which makes searching for a certain term in multiple videos or audio recordings quick and easy. The feature may slow down the search process a bit and does require OneNote to index your audio and video while your computer is idle. However, when it comes to using a few watts of electricity while you're off doing something else versus having to watch or at least scan through entire multiple videos to find the key-words manually, without question this feature can be crazily useful.

✔ OneNote's presence on multiple types of devices allows users to share notes between smartphones and devices — be it via Android's Beam feature, Bluetooth, or e-mail. Nexus devices aren't the only smartphones to have NFC, either. Windows Phone 8 devices do as well, although at the time of this writing, iPhone doesn't.

Whether the Beam feature will work between Windows Phone and Android phones in the future is dubious given the parent companies' publicly stated loathing of one another.

Taking OneNote to Work

OneNote has amazing uses in the workplace, from medical offices, to sales organizations, to field work, or to any organization that has meetings. The following sections give examples of how OneNote can transform your work environment.

Tracking charts in medical offices

For the most part, medical offices probably don't use OneNote — yet. Medical charts typically are created and maintained using specific industry-created software. However, many clinics currently use paper notes that are eventually transcribed onto charts, and that's where OneNote can shine.

The following fictional example is about John, a doctor in a 400-bed facility for elderly veterans. He and other doctors make rounds every morning, meet with team members from other specialties, and work the rest of the day diagnosing and treating symptoms and ailments as they occur or become evident.

7:45 a.m.: John walks into his office to prepare for his 8 a.m. status meeting with the treatment team for his unit of 15 elderly veterans. With ease, he settles into his chair, puts his Surface Pro flat on the table, and jots down a few notes after creating a new page named according to today's date in a section named by the week in a notebook named after the month. He knows you can have as many sections as you want in a notebook, but he prefers organization by month, so that's what he goes with. John accesses his voicemail, turns on the speakerphone, opens OneNote for Windows 8 on Surface, creates a new page named Voicemail, and scribbles a few notes on the screen with his digital pen while he listens. He uses his favorite highlighter pen to highlight notes he needs to discuss in the 8 a.m. meeting.

After reviewing his voicemail, he plugs Surface into his HD monitor with a mini HDMI cable and logs in to his Outlook e-mail to see what's new. His desktop is automatically extended, and he keeps OneNote on the Surface while viewing Outlook on the monitor. He opens a new page called Daily E-Mails and jots down some information, sends a few of the e-mails to the page via the Send to OneNote feature in Outlook, and again uses his favorite pen to highlight key issues in the e-mails that need to be discussed at the meeting. He places check boxes next to the items he needs to discuss. When he finishes the note, he unplugs the HDMI cable from the Surface and grabs the tablet, turns off his monitor, and heads to the meeting.

8:00 a.m.: John and other team members discuss the happenings on the unit with the 15 elderly veterans they're taking care of. During the meeting, John scrolls through his Voicemail and Daily E-Mails pages, addressing each item and checking off the boxes next to each one after discussing them. Later today — it's Tuesday — is the day for team meetings between all disciplines and seven of the 15 individuals being cared for on the unit (the other eight are scheduled for Thursday). He sighs quietly as the morning meeting begins — he doesn't see a lot of sunlight during team days.

An administrative assistant sits at a desktop computer that projects to a large screen on the wall. As she takes notes using her keyboard and OneNote 2013, she creates Outlook follow-up tasks for the people at the meeting. John, for example, has a new task today: He needs to determine which patients for whom he has prescribed a heart medication that has a new black-box cancer warning attached to it; then he needs to look at the pros and cons of switching the medication for each individual patient.

When the meeting is over, the administrative assistant will go back to her desk, finish formatting the note page, and e-mail it to all members of the team.

2:00 p.m.: *The team meeting for the patient, Mr. Campbell, is just starting. Present are his recreation therapist, social worker, nurse, psychologist, psychiatrist, the unit dietician, and John, who is his medical doctor. Present also is Jeena, the administrative assistant. Jeena opens up OneNote 2013, which projects onto a large screen on the wall. Everyone can see the notebook's name — Campbell, H. 03142 — the section named after the month and year, a subsection of the week, and pages within it named Rec Therapy, Social Work, Dietician, Dental (the dentist is present at only one team meeting every three months, unless otherwise needed), Psychiatry, Nursing, and Medical.*

Mr. Campbell is brought in after his treatment plan is up on the screen and in order. In turn, each treatment team member presents her weekly update on the patient, getting feedback from Mr. Campbell as necessary. Jeena creates Outlook tasks as necessary for follow-up for the individual — for example, John is tasked to ping the facility's optometrist to see when Mr. Campbell's glasses, which were ordered three weeks ago, will be in.

3:30 p.m.: *John gets back to his office and hooks up to his monitor again, this time propping up the Surface on its kickstand and laying out his Type Cover keyboard — he doesn't like the Touch Cover at all because the buttons really aren't buttons; there's no key "press." Via the extended display, he views Outlook on the main monitor and OneNote for Windows 8 on his Surface Pro.*

He types his e-mails as necessary, with the treatment plans for his various patients open on the HD monitor as he does so — he's concerned with only the Medical page in each plan. After each e-mail he needs to write, he marks his Outlook task complete, which notifies any team member who needs to know that the task is complete. He also opens up his note page from the morning meeting and checks off the tasks he'd jotted down himself, and in so doing realizes he still hasn't pinged the Social Work department to see who is covering for the unit social worker going on vacation Thursday. He does so via phone — he tends to use the phone with people he actually enjoys talking to, and Nancy, the chief of social work, is quite a hoot — and then checks the box off in OneNote. By this time, it's nearly 5 p.m., and John is exhausted. He turns off his equipment and leaves his office for the night.

Following are some keys to take away from John's story:

✔ OneNote isn't likely to become the software for medical charts, but it can easily be the means by which to note needed changes before transferring those changes from OneNote to official medical documentation.

✔ OneNote notes can be on a shared server so that everyone who needs to can access a document, such as a treatment team plan, at will. When I worked at a state hospital as a clinical social worker, my treatment team used Word, not OneNote, and it was a painful process because each treatment plan was typically an extremely long document, especially when individuals had been at the hospital for awhile. With OneNote, those treatment plans could have been pages within sections, with one page for each discipline.

Word is best used for documents that require very precise formatting, *not* for multi-disciplinary treatment team plans. When working as a clinical social worker in a state hospital, with Word I had to scroll through agonizingly long documents, hunting for social work-related items that were set apart from items from other disciplines only by a certain number code. Worse, individuals from other disciplines could accidentally screw up what I wrote — not all clinicians are tech savvy. With a OneNote-based treatment plan, I could have easily accessed my "share" of the document in OneNote by opening the notebook for the individual, opening the section including the month and week I needed, and then accessing the Social Work page for that day without having to slog through other disciplines' items to find mine. Most notably, *other disciplines' representatives would be much less likely to botch up my page if it were a separate page from theirs.*

✔ Outlook tasks are very useful for organizations using Outlook and the Exchange Server behind it, and OneNote integrates nicely with Outlook tasks. At the same time, using check boxes, To Do items, and other tags, you can complement the use of Outlook tasks by creating your own unofficial tasks using OneNote tags.

Simplifying corporate meetings

Corporations tend to use Office a lot, and because OneNote can accept content from the major Office apps, notes from meetings can be richer and more diverse in terms of content. Furthermore, notes can be collaborated on and finalized in the meeting.

The following fictional story is about Brandon and his sales team as they finalize changes to their product line of video games.

Brandon grabs his Surface Pro and walks to the meeting room, taking his customary seat near Bonnie the administrative assistant at the head of the conference table. Bonnie is just finishing setting up the conference call with the marketing and sales teams in New York. The chatter from the large screen at the other end of the room is jovial — it's the first week back after Christmas and not only is everyone rested, but also it's common knowledge that sales of their latest game "Furious Fowl" was stellar over the Christmas season.

As the meeting starts moments later, Brandon says "Hello New York, Sydney, and Tokyo!" Chatter is heard from the other locations as they reply in kind.

Brandon brings up a PowerPoint document and flips through the first slides, essentially laying out the format for the meeting and informing the group about key sales figures. He then brings up an Excel document on his Surface and focuses the screen on a particular chart. Murmurs of approval are heard all around.

Bonnie, working on a desktop built in to the conference room, silently accesses the PowerPoint slides and drops them into a page in OneNote under a section named after the meeting data and time. She copies the PowerPoint slides into one page, adds some space under one of the slides that is relevant to the Excel chart Brandon is showing, and pastes the chart there. In between slides, she types notes based on what Brandon is saying about other folks' responsibilities to prepare for the game's sequel, "Furious Fowl Timbuktu." In another tab, she's already running a video recording of the meeting in case she needs to refer to it later.

Brandon has access to the same note that Bonnie is working on and brings it up on his Surface as people discuss the information in the Excel chart. With his pen, he marks up what Bonnie has typed, adding and changing items as needed. As she catches up, she goes back through the note and makes his changes in the formatted text. Because her desktop setup has a touchscreen, if there is too much writing, she can circle it with her pen, press and hold on it, and choose Ink to Text to turn it into text.

*Brandon brings up a flowchart in Visio and shares it with Bonnie.
Bonnie immediately inserts the chart into OneNote, right-clicks it with
her mouse, and chooses Edit, which brings the chart up in Visio for
editing. She shares with the group, and the Visio flowchart replaces
the view of the attendees on the display at the end of the room.
Discussion begins about dates for having a demo ready for the new
game, dates for marketing, and other deadlines. Attendees make
comments, and Bonnie makes changes in Visio accordingly. Bonnie
saves the file and closes Visio, and the flowchart in OneNote automatically updates with the changes.*

*As the meeting closes, attendees comment on the note's contents, and
Bonnie makes changes accordingly. When she's finished, she clicks
the E-Mail Note button on the Home tab in OneNote 2013, brings
up the Outlook contact that includes all attendees, adds a couple
more names, and sends the file. All attendees have the note in their
inboxes before getting up and leaving the meeting.*

Following are a few comments on how OneNote saved some time
and effort:

- ✔ OneNote's ability to include information from other Office
  apps is quite powerful. Not only can you actually launch the
  content in Visio from within OneNote, but also the flow chart
  updates itself in OneNote when saved in Visio, so you don't
  have to insert the first version of the file, delete the first version
  after it changes, and insert a second, edited version of the file.

- ✔ Having OneNote on a touchscreen PC that also has a keyboard
  and mouse and a digital pen lets the user utilize whatever interface makes the most sense at a given time. No one can determine this but the user, and the various interfaces allow for the
  most fluid, efficient user interface for the person doing the work.

- ✔ Sharing the note across different locations and editing it once,
  while everyone is still viewing it, saves bandwidth. Compare,
  for example, the one e-mail Bonnie sent at the end of the meeting to the "old school" process, where you would transcribe
  notes from paper, e-mail a draft to everyone after a meeting,
  wait for people to e-mail changes back, field and incorporate
  requested changes — after clarifying requests with people
  who didn't quite get what was said — then e-mail a revised
  second draft to everyone, field *those* changes from everyone
  again via e-mail, and at last, send out a final version. The
  revised process with a single e-mail sent before the meeting is
  even over saves company bandwidth — and Bonnie's sanity
  and workflow. Furthermore, given that the final note is finalized and sent to everyone before they even get up from their
  seats, a lot of time is saved for everyone.

Field work

OneNote Web App allows people to edit notes whether they have OneNote 2013 or not. People can also use the app to view who makes what changes, and people in different time zones can make changes when it suits them and others can view them later.

The following fictional account is about Allison, who travels all over the world for a multi-national car company to assess business operations.

May 20, 7:00 a.m.: Allison arrives in Tokyo to visit her company's local car manufacturing plant. She starts a note while in her hotel room so it's ready for her to jot down her assessments.

9:00 a.m.: Allison visits the local plant and, Surface Pro in hand, walks down the assembly line looking for inconsistencies and issues with timeliness. She notices that the machine responsible for installing windshield wipers seems slower than usual and is a little choppy. She records a brief video from OneNote, makes some notes below it using her pen, and moves along.

May 21, 8:30 a.m.: After showering and eating, Allison logs in to her OneNote app and notices that her colleague in Detroit has made notes alongside hers. She toggles Recent Edits on the History tab in OneNote 2013 (her compatriot in Detroit is using OneNote Web App, but she doesn't notice a difference other than his notes are text, not ink) and notes to herself that he made these changes while she was at dinner — and that he did so an hour before he was even supposed to be at work, so she makes a mental note to complement him on his dedication.

Allison incorporates his notes into her final report and then copies and pastes the entire note into a Word document, formatting the text as necessary for a standard memo to department heads in Detroit, who prefer Word's memo templates for final memos. She sends the memo on via e-mail and shuts down her Surface as she packs and readies herself for a trip to Germany, where she will perform the whole process again at a plant in Bonn.

Following are some notes on how Allison's experience was improved by her technology:

 ✔ Because she had a Surface and was using OneNote with a pen, she was able to take notes right on her device as she walked through the plant, even recording a video with it.

✔ OneNote Web App allowed her colleague to review and add to her notes even without OneNote.

✔ Showing revisions allowed Allison to see when exactly her colleague worked on the file.

Simplifying Your Life with OneNote at Home

OneNote isn't just useful in professional situations; it can make your home life a heck of a lot easier, too. The following sections describe ways OneNote can enhance your life at home.

Prescriptions

If you have any prescriptions, you may find them a pain to deal with, and this becomes exponentially true the more prescriptions you have. If you manage prescriptions for a family, life can become even harder when juggling prescription codes and bar codes on bottles — God forbid you forget them at home while you're out and need to get them. The potential hassles are many and varied. The following fictional account is about Anthony, whose wife has cancer and is currently bed-ridden and whose children each have at least two prescriptions.

The last time Anthony went to the pharmacy to refill meds for his family, he forgot one of his wife's pain meds, resulting in a second trip in the middle of the night when his wife had one less pain pill than he thought she had. Today, his day off, he decides to solve the problem with his new Surface Pro and OneNote.

Anthony grabs prescription documentation for everyone in his family, including his, and lines them up on the kitchen table. He starts a new OneNote notebook called Family Needs and a new section called Meds. Person by person, he uses the Surface Pro's front camera to snap a picture of the key page that shows the medicine's barcode, fill date, and prescribing physician.

A week later, his wife calls him at work and asks him to refill a medicine for her and their daughter. Effortlessly, he brings out his Surface and his Android phone. Bringing up his wife's note page, he finds the med in question and uses the barcode scanner in his pharmacy's Android app to instantly scan the med's barcode. The app processes the refill, and he taps a couple times to change the pickup time from tomorrow to today. He does the same for his daughter using the scanned documentation for her meds. Then, on his way home, he rolls through the pharmacy's drive-thru window, congratulating him-self on the significant time he saved — not to mention the extra trip he won't have to make in the middle of the night.

Here are a few notes on how Anthony's devices saved him time:

✔ OneNote's ability to capture images and instantly insert them into a note saved Anthony from having to scan and import images of the prescription pages.

✔ Anthony's phone enabled him to scan barcodes right from his tablet screen and instantly request prescription refills from the pharmacy without a phone call.

Recipes and grocery lists

Recipes and grocery lists on paper are a pain to deal with. Which pocket did you put the list in — or did you put it in a pocket at all? Do you take the whole recipe with you or transcribe each ingre-dient required and the amount required onto paper and hope it doesn't get lost in your pockets or purse? With OneNote, such wor-ries are no more — recipes can become grocery lists in seconds and can reside in a single, obvious location on your smartphone, which you're never without.

The following scenario describes Samantha as she uses OneNote to turn a single recipe into a grocery list with a few taps, instead of transcribing it by hand and haggling with little paper notes.

Samantha is hosting a family dinner for her in-laws, and her hubby really wants her to try and make his late grandmother's recipe for chocolate mush cake. He has forwarded the recipe to her, which he acquired from his aunt via an e-mail with a copy scanned from an old paper copy of the recipe.

Samantha sits down at her desktop PC and opens OneNote 2013 and her e-mail app. She saves the scanned copy of the paper recipe, drops the image into OneNote, right-clicks the image, and chooses Copy Text from Picture. Below the image, which she decides to keep in the note for reference, she pastes the text from the image. Next to each of the ingredients, she adds a check box. She shuts down her computer — OneNote saves and syncs to her SkyDrive automatically — and drives to the store.

At the store, Samantha brings up her smartphone, logs in to the store's Wi-Fi, and opens OneNote on her iPhone. She finds the page with the recipe and taps the check box next to each of the ingredients as she puts it in her basket. When all ingredients are checked off, she knows she's got what she needs.

Paper notes suck. Transcribing recipe lists into ingredients lists suck. With OneNote, Samantha doesn't need to do either. Enough said.

Dictating ideas

Ideas come and go, but they don't have to go into the ether just because you forget them. If you have a smartphone with OneNote on it, you can easily make sure you never forget a great idea again.

The following brief scenario shows James dictating notes into his OneNote Mobile for Android.

Tom is a programmer for Innitech Inc. — and a would-be inventor — so he knows the value of ideas and feels a loss with each one he can't remember. He has decided to use his smartphone and OneNote Mobile to never forget an idea again.

One night while waiting at a bus stop, Tom has a brilliant idea that he knows will make him millions. Grabbing his smartphone, he opens OneNote, taps to create a new unfiled note, and taps into the note to summon the keyboard. He taps the microphone icon, and his phone changes displays to tell him to Speak Now. He does so and watches as the text appears in the note. He finishes a thought and corrects the few words that didn't get translated properly into text and then closes the phone.

On his way home from the bus stop, Tom is mugged by a gang wearing granny masks and carrying baseball bats. Among the things they take is his smartphone. One of the thugs knocks him in the head with a bat, and Tom takes a nasty spill off a concrete staircase, and as a result, suffers a major concussion.

Later, Tom awakes from a six-week coma. When he gets home after six more weeks of agonizing therapy, he logs in to OneNote Web App and sees his brilliant idea before him, untouched. Thankful for OneNote's auto-saving and sync feature, he begins writing a proposal for his brilliant idea — a "Jump to Conclusions Pad" that you can jump from one conclusion to another after asking it a question. He later becomes a millionaire.

Thugs aside — okay, I was ready for a little drama in this chapter — the ability to dictate to OneNote Mobile means Tom doesn't have to carry a miniature recorder in addition to a phone. And yes, if the phone goes bye-bye for some reason, the note is intact thanks to OneNote's auto-saving and syncing. Whether you drop the phone in water, smash it in frustration when your significant other tells you to kick rocks on Valentine's Day, drop it off a cliff to see just how durable Gorilla Glass 18 really is, or relinquish it under duress to creepy granny-masked muggers, OneNote saves and syncs your notes automatically so that they're accessible whenever you access SkyDrive again.

Job application information

How irritating is it to have to fill out apps on the spot and not be able to remember all the details about your previous employers, the dates you worked, and so on? So don't do it. Type, write, paste, or otherwise get that key information into a note in OneNote and access it from your phone wherever you are. This one's so simple it really doesn't require a scenario. Just make sure you password-protect that note so that no one can easily get this information if you lost your phone. 'Nuff said.

Part IV
The Part of Tens

Enjoy an additional OneNote 2013 "Part of Tens" chapter online at www.dummies.com/extras/onenote2013.

In this part . . .

✔ Learn about some killer uses for OneNote.

✔ Check out some great OneNote resources.

✔ Try out some OneNote add-ins.

✔ Find out how OneNote can save your butt.

Chapter 12

Ten (or So) Resources and Add-Ins for OneNote

*O*neNote wasn't the most popular application until recently, having more of a cult following than being known as a go-to app. As such, resources for OneNote are not many at this point, and some of those that exist — even those from Microsoft — aren't always updated as often as you would hope. Still, there are some good resources for OneNote out there, and this chapter outlines more than ten of them.

OneNote 2013 For Dummies Online

For Dummies books are more and more about integrating content with the web, and this book is no exception. Because I'm essentially a social media geek, you have no lack of resources online for this book; whether your social media tastes include Facebook, Twitter, or the new, powerful Google+ platform, this book has got you covered.

Facebook page

For Facebook, I created a page so that I can share tips and tricks with you, as well as more on resources and add-ons as I find them, after the book is released. You can also engage there with me, trade information, and even just socialize with other OneNote geeks. You can find the Facebook page at the following URL:

```
www.facebook.com/onenotefordummies
```

Google+ page

Google+ is a relatively new social media service that ties into Google search results. I created a Google+ page and community (see the next section) for the same reason as I did the Facebook page: to post information and resources for OneNote for readers after the book is in print. Consider it the book that keeps on giving! Check out the Google+ page at the following URL:

```
https://plus.google.com/106026481219308555200/posts
```

Google+ community

The difference between a Google+ page and community is that a page is run by one person, and although other people can comment, they cannot create new posts like they can in a community. Communities have moderators who keep control of members and posts, and members can create posts under various moderator-created categories. Check out the Google+ community and hang out at the following URL:

```
https://plus.google.com/communities/
113924971379976513445
```

Twitter account

Twitter's 140-character limit makes it perfect for quick shout-outs for tips, resources, and add-ins as well as for interacting with other Twitter followers. Follow @OneNoteFD on Twitter to check out tweets from me and retweets from OneNote users and related Twitter accounts, such as those listed in the "OneNote on Twitter" section later in this chapter.

Microsoft's OneNote Blog

Although as of this writing the blog isn't updated very often — as of now it's been nearly six months since its last update — the site does have a good repository of webinars, tips, videos, and how-to articles that give you information about OneNote from the horse's mouth. Chances are that Microsoft will eventually update the site and perhaps start doing so more often, so this is a good blog to keep bookmarked and access every so often to see if anything new is up.

```
http://blogs.office.com/b/microsoft-onenote
```

Office.com OneNote Templates

Even though the site currently includes *zero* templates specifically for OneNote 2013, chances are this will change in the near future. As of this writing, OneNote 2013 has just been released, and templates are likely to show up on the site at some point. That said, there are plenty of OneNote 2010 and OneNote 2007 templates available for you to use, most of which probably work just fine with OneNote 2013.

```
http://office.microsoft.com/en-us/templates/
results.aspx?qu=onenote&av=zsc
```

The best advice I can give you in regard to using templates for OneNote 2007 or 2010 is to just try them. Download them from the site, extract them to your chosen location, and open them and work with them. I did just that with the Wedding Planner template for OneNote 2007, and as you can see in Figure 12-1, the template opened just fine in OneNote 2013. Most likely they don't support the latest features of OneNote, but that doesn't mean you can't add those features yourself.

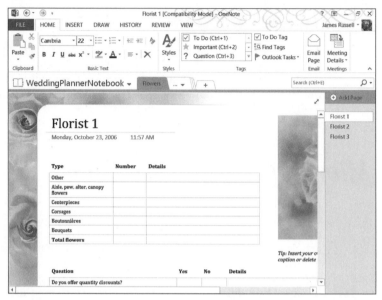

Figure 12-1: The OneNote 2007 Wedding Planner template in OneNote 2013.

OneNote on Facebook

If you want to Like OneNote on Facebook, write on the wall for the application, and find tips and comments from others who dig OneNote, you can find OneNote on Facebook at the following URL:

`www.facebook.com/MicrosoftOneNote`

Microsoft updates this page — at least as of this writing — more often than it does so on Twitter at the official Office blog, which are both described later in the chapter.

OneNote on Twitter

Twitter is home to two major OneNote-related accounts from Microsoft. @Office is updated often and includes some OneNote-related posts. @msonenote, the official Microsoft OneNote Twitter account, tweets at least major updates to the software, as of this writing.

Engineering OneNote Blog

Despite the blog's name, it includes information about some of the more killer features of OneNote, as well as new add-ins. Find the blog at the following URL:

```
http://blogs.msdn.com/b/descapa
```

OneNote Testing Blog

The one Microsoft-led blog that is actually updated on a regular basis, this blog is written by Microsoft OneNote tester John Guin. He includes a lot of information about OneNote resources as well as information on add-ins. You can access Guin's blog at the following URL:

```
http://blogs.msdn.com/b/johnguin
```

Clip to OneNote Add-In

Clip to OneNote is a browser extension for Firefox, Chrome, and Opera that lets you clip web pages or fully formatted portions of pages to OneNote within your browser. The extension also has a version for Mozilla Thunderbird. IE already has these capabilities, and the extension's author simply wanted to add the capability to Firefox. The add-on adds a menu item to the context menu in your browser (or Thunderbird when viewing a web page) so that you can simply right-click a web page or selection of a web page and choose to clip it to OneNote.

Clip to OneNote is not exactly the easiest add-on to install; essentially, you will have to download two extensions — a "listener" and the actual extension — before the add-on will work. You also have to set a communication port for Listener to listen on. If you have no idea what this refers to, the default port 2866 should be fine. If there is a conflict, the add-on should notify you and come up with a different port for you to try.

The main page for the add-on is `http://web.madharasan.com/projects/clip-to-onenote`

You can find Clip to OneNote on Facebook at `www.facebook.com/clip.to.onenote`.

Onetastic and OneCalendar

Onetastic is a comprehensive add-on for OneNote that includes a lot of really cool features, including those giving you the ability to do the following:

- ✔ Create menu or desktop shortcuts to your most-used notes.
- ✔ Crop photos within OneNote.
- ✔ Customize styles in OneNote like you can in Word.
- ✔ Use macros in OneNote for functions like you can in Excel.

OneCalendar is a separate application from OneNote that allows you to view your notes on a calendar based on the date they were created or updated.

Both Onetastic and OneCalendar are free and available from the following URL:

```
http://omeratay.com/onetastic/?r=download
```

Outline and Outline+

Outline is a third-party version of OneNote for iPad that includes a lot more features than OneNote for iOS does, as of this writing. Outline+ includes more features — including ink, according to the Outline website — and allows you to create more than the 30 notes you're limited to with Outline, but you have to pay $14.99 for it. Gorillized Corporation, the makers of Outline, have also announced that a version will be released soon for Mac OS X that will allow viewing only on a Mac.

You can find Outline here: `http://outline.ws/features`.

Office Labs and OneNote Blog

Microsoft Developer Network (MSDN) is made up of engineers that use Microsoft technologies to develop applications and other engineering-related settings. Although not updated often, at least as of the time of this writing, this blog is run by a Microsoft employee Chris Pratley and has some good OneNote content.

Here's the URL: `http://blogs.msdn.com/b/chris_pratley/`.

Chapter 13

Ten Killer Tips for OneNote

*I*n earlier chapters of the book, I describe a lot of cool tips for things you can do with OneNote, especially in Chapter 11 where I discuss various scenarios describing using OneNote in the real world. In this chapter, I describe ten tips for OneNote to further show you how useful the app can be in simplifying your life.

Backing Up Important Data

Accessing notes from wherever you are is discussed to some degree in other chapters, but it bears repeating and perhaps expounding on a bit. Here are a few examples of how OneNote backups can save your rear:

✔ You leave on a trip across the country, and magically your carry-on bag goes missing. Luckily, you still have your phone — and your itinerary. You find your plane with just a few minutes to spare — but you find it and are on it. Solid.

✔ You forget to bring and review your resume before that killer important interview, but you backed it up on OneNote and have your iPad with you. Heck, you may even impress your boss-to-be just by having your resume on your iPad!

✔ Left your report — due today — on the counter at home when you decided to grab that health-nut bar for breakfast. Home is at least an hour away, and there's no way to get the printed copy to your teacher in time. Got it in OneNote? Print it in the school lab, and you're square.

The list could go on forever, but you get the idea. Backing up your important documents on OneNote and SkyDrive is a good idea, mmkay?

Accessing Entire Office Documents on iOS or Android

At the time of this writing at least, OneNote is the only Office app on Android. Although you may not be able to work much with other Office apps in OneNote on Android or iOS, you can at the very least access and view them. Have important data in Excel you need on the run, and your laptop isn't accessible? View it on your Android or iOS tablet.

If you want the document in perfect visual form, simply include it as a printout instead of pasting the document in, and it will look just like the document in its native app in OneNote. It won't be at all editable, but you will be able to see it just fine.

If the Office file is Word, Excel, or PowerPoint, you can also upload it to your SkyDrive and access it via the appropriate web app using SkyDrive in a web browser on your device and actually be able to edit it, albeit with a subset of the options of the full Office app.

Dictating Notes Straight to Text

As I discuss in Chapter 7, the Android version of OneNote, as of this writing, doesn't allow you to record voice notes, but you can tap the Android microphone button on the keyboard and talk to OneNote, translating your speech straight into text. If this is what you want in the first place, you can look at this as a feature instead of a missing option! Hopefully, Android's version of OneNote Mobile will support taking audio and/or video notes in the future, but also hopefully this particular "feature" won't go away because frankly it can be pretty useful when compared to manually typing a dictated audio note.

Retrieving Text from Images

Of course, I mention this topic in other chapters, but it, too, is worth mentioning in this chapter because it's such a killer feature. Simply right-click a photo or image in OneNote 2013 and choose Copy Text from Picture, and you've got the text from the image on your clipboard.

Make your screenshot as high-quality as possible to ensure that you get the actual text from the image. The feature also doesn't work as well if your image is too dark or if the text is in a funky font. Even in those cases, though, you probably can get at least *some* of the text from the image and avoid at least a bit of retyping.

Grabbing a Screen Clipping and Marking It Up

As mentioned in Chapter 4, you can snap screenshots using the OneNote 2013 Clipping Tool. After dropping the screenshot into OneNote, using your pen you can use Office's ink features to mark up the image. This can be useful in any situation where you want to add notes to an image and share it; say if you're working on developing a website and want to show your collaborators what you feel needs to change with the current iteration of the site.

Of course, you can use actual text if you don't have access to a PC capable of digital pen technology like Surface Pro. You can even use your mouse pointer as a pen to draw if your "mouse handwriting" is good enough.

Marking Up Documents with a Pen

If you have access to a digital pen-capable PC like Microsoft's Surface Pro, marking up documents in OneNote is simple. However, if you want to retain some semblance of the formatting, it's best done by including a printout of the document rather than pasting the content of a document into the note page.

If you have access on the digital pen-capable PC to other Office 2013 apps, in some cases, you can use the pen to mark up the documents in that app, as is the case with Word 2013. Other apps are pickier; for example you can write a new e-mail using the pen and ink, but you can't reply to a non-ink message using the pen.

Copying Links to Specific Paragraphs

If you want to link people to a specific part of a OneNote page, simply right-click or press and hold on the paragraph or note container that you want to link to and choose the Copy Link to Paragraph option to copy a link to that note and paragraph to your PC's clipboard. You can then paste the link wherever you want.

Searching Text in Images

If you drop an image into OneNote and want the text in it to be searchable later, right-click or press and hold on the image and choose Make Text in Image Searchable and choose the appropriate language from the list.

Docking OneNote to the Desktop

If you're using OneNote quite a bit and want it to effectively sit beneath all other windows open on your screen (so you don't have to haggle with selecting it from the Windows taskbar), you can. Simply select the View tab and click or tap the Dock to Desktop button, and OneNote will dock itself onto your desktop, sitting beneath all open windows. Other windows will move a bit, so you can always see OneNote on the right side of your screen.

Creating Outlook 2013 Tasks from OneNote

The Home tab in OneNote 2013 includes an Outlook Tasks drop-down list that you can access to create tasks for various time frames. The list includes options to delete a task or to open the task in Outlook. The task automatically adds itself to the bottom of your list of tasks in Outlook as long as you have Outlook 2013 set up and configured on the same PC you're using OneNote 2013 on.

You don't have to start a new task and then add the task information; you can simply select an existing item and then choose from the drop-down list to immediately make that item a task.

Index

• T •

• Z •

Notes

Notes

Apple & Mac

iPad For Dummies,
5th Edition
978-1-118-49823-1

iPhone 5 For Dummies,
6th Edition
978-1-118-35201-4

MacBook For
Dummies, 4th Edition
978-1-118-20920-2

OS X Mountain Lion
For Dummies
978-1-118-39418-2

Blogging & Social Media

Facebook For
Dummies, 4th Edition
978-1-118-09562-1

Mom Blogging
For Dummies
978-1-118-03843-7

Pinterest For Dummies
978-1-118-32800-2

WordPress For
Dummies, 5th Edition
978-1-118-38318-6

Business

Commodities For
Dummies, 2nd Edition
978-1-118-01687-9

Investing For
Dummies, 6th Edition
978-0-470-90545-6

Personal Finance
For Dummies,
7th Edition
978-1-118-11785-9

QuickBooks 2013
For Dummies
978-1-118-35641-8

Small Business
Marketing Kit For
Dummies, 3rd Edition
978-1-118-31183-7

Careers

Job Interviews For
Dummies, 4th Edition
978-1-118-11290-8

Job Searching with
Social Media
For Dummies
978-0-470-93072-4

Personal Branding
For Dummies
978-1-118-11792-7

Resumes For
Dummies, 6th Edition
978-0-470-87361-8

Success as a Mediator
For Dummies
978-1-118-07862-4

Diet & Nutrition

Belly Fat Diet
For Dummies
978-1-118-34585-6

Eating Clean
For Dummies
978-1-118-00013-7

Nutrition For
Dummies, 5th Edition
978-0-470-93231-5

Digital Photography

Digital Photography
For Dummies,
7th Edition
978-1-118-09203-3

Digital SLR Cameras
& Photography For
Dummies, 4th Edition
978-1-118-14489-3

Photoshop Elements 11
For Dummies
978-1-118-40821-6

Gardening

Herb Gardening For
Dummies, 2nd Edition
978-0-470-61778-6

Vegetable Gardening
For Dummies,
2nd Edition
978-0-470-49870-5

Health

Anti-Inflammation Diet
For Dummies
978-1-118-02381-5

Diabetes For Dummies,
3rd Edition
978-0-470-27086-8

Living Paleo
For Dummies
978-1-118-29405-5

Hobbies

Beekeeping
For Dummies
978-0-470-43065-1

eBay For Dummies,
7th Edition
978-1-118-09806-6

Raising Chickens
For Dummies
978-0-470-46544-8

Wine For Dummies,
5th Edition
978-1-118-28872-6

Writing Young Adult
Fiction For Dummies
978-0-470-94954-2

Language & Foreign Language

500 Spanish Verbs
For Dummies
978-1-118-02382-2

English Grammar For
Dummies, 2nd Edition
978-0-470-54664-2

French All-in One
For Dummies
978-1-118-22815-9

German Essentials
For Dummies
978-1-118-18422-6

Italian For Dummies,
2nd Edition
978-1-118-00465-4

 Available in print and e-book formats.

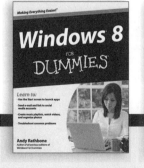

Available wherever books are sold. For more information or to order direct: U.S. customers visit www.Dummies.com or call 1-877-762-2974.U.K. customers visit www.Wileyeurope.com or call (0) 1243 843291.
Canadian customers visit www.Wiley.ca or call 1-800-567-4797.

Connect with us online at www.facebook.com/fordummies or @fordummies

Math & Science

Algebra I For Dummies, 2nd Edition
978-0-470-55964-2

Anatomy and Physiology For Dummies, 2nd Edition
978-0-470-92326-9

Astronomy For Dummies, 3rd Edition
978-1-118-37697-3

Biology For Dummies, 2nd Edition
978-0-470-59875-7

Chemistry For Dummies, 2nd Edition
978-1-1180-0730-3

Pre-Algebra Essentials For Dummies
978-0-470-61838-7

Microsoft Office

Excel 2013 For Dummies
978-1-118-51012-4

Office 2013 All-in-One For Dummies
978-1-118-51636-2

PowerPoint 2013 For Dummies
978-1-118-50253-2

Word 2013 For Dummies
978-1-118-49123-2

Music

Blues Harmonica For Dummies
978-1-118-25269-7

Guitar For Dummies, 3rd Edition
978-1-118-11554-1

iPod & iTunes For Dummies, 10th Edition
978-1-118-50864-0

Programming

Android Application Development For Dummies, 2nd Edition
978-1-118-38710-8

iOS 6 Application Development For Dummies
978-1-118-50880-0

Java For Dummies, 5th Edition
978-0-470-37173-2

Religion & Inspiration

The Bible For Dummies
978-0-7645-5296-0

Buddhism For Dummies, 2nd Edition
978-1-118-02379-2

Catholicism For Dummies, 2nd Edition
978-1-118-07778-8

Self-Help & Relationships

Bipolar Disorder For Dummies, 2nd Edition
978-1-118-33882-7

Meditation For Dummies, 3rd Edition
978-1-118-29144-3

Seniors

Computers For Seniors For Dummies, 3rd Edition
978-1-118-11553-4

iPad For Seniors For Dummies, 5th Edition
978-1-118-49708-1

Social Security For Dummies
978-1-118-20573-0

Smartphones & Tablets

Android Phones For Dummies
978-1-118-16952-0

Kindle Fire HD For Dummies
978-1-118-42223-6

NOOK HD For Dummies, Portable Edition
978-1-118-39498-4

Surface For Dummies
978-1-118-49634-3

Test Prep

ACT For Dummies, 5th Edition
978-1-118-01259-8

ASVAB For Dummies, 3rd Edition
978-0-470-63760-9

GRE For Dummies, 7th Edition
978-0-470-88921-3

Officer Candidate Tests, For Dummies
978-0-470-59876-4

Physician's Assistant Exam For Dummies
978-1-118-11556-5

Series 7 Exam For Dummies
978-0-470-09932-2

Windows 8

Windows 8 For Dummies
978-1-118-13461-0

Windows 8 For Dummies, Book + DVD Bundle
978-1-118-27167-4

Windows 8 All-in-One For Dummies
978-1-118-11920-4

 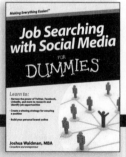  

𝑒 Available in print and e-book formats.

Take Dummies with you everywhere you go!

Whether you're excited about e-books, want more from the web, must have your mobile apps, or swept up in social media, Dummies makes everything easier .